INTRODUCTION

High above a crowded political rally, a hidden figure aims his rifle and squeezes the trigger. . . . The smiling President reaches out to greet a well-wisher and receives a knife in his heart. . . . That is the pattern of assassination—sudden, deadly, treacherous—an act which sends shockwaves rippling down through history.

In this compelling study of the world's most significant crime, a well-known journalist analyzes the deadly phenomenon which has stalked our leaders through the ages. In re-creating over 10 successful and attempted assassinations, the author strips bare the shadowy world of the political murderer, and reveals the terrifying vulnerability of his victim.

He begins with the legendary 'Old Man of the Mountains'—the religious despot whose hashish-eating followers gave their name to the act of public and political murder. He goes on to examine the slaying of Marat by Charlotte Corday, and the numerous attempts on the life of General de Gaulle. Then, in a nightmarish roll-call of the slain, the author explores assassinations to the present day: Rasputin—the power behind the Russian Throne; Trotsky—sacrificed in the Stalinist blood-purge; Verwoerd—victim of his own repression; Hitler—fated to survive a dozen death plots; the Kennedys—a family cursed.

A lucid text and nearly 100 photographs capture some of the most heart-stopping events in history. The reader will be both fascinated and frightened as the grim saga unfolds, for one fact becomes clear—the spectre of the assassin is always present in the halls of the famous and powerful.

For Heaven's sake, let us sit upon the ground
And tell sad stories of the death of kings:
How some have been depos'd; some slain in war;
Some haunted by the ghosts they have depos'd;
Some poisoned by their wives; some sleeping kill'd;
All murder'd.
—*Richard II*, Act III
William Shakespeare

Every country has its own constitution; ours is
absolutism tempered by assassination.
—An intelligent Russian
quoted by Count Munster in
*Political Sketches of the
State of Europe, 1814-1867*

Assassination is the perquisite of kings.
—King Umberto I of Italy

Assassination never changed the history of the world.
—Benjamin Disraeli, in a
speech on the death of Lincoln

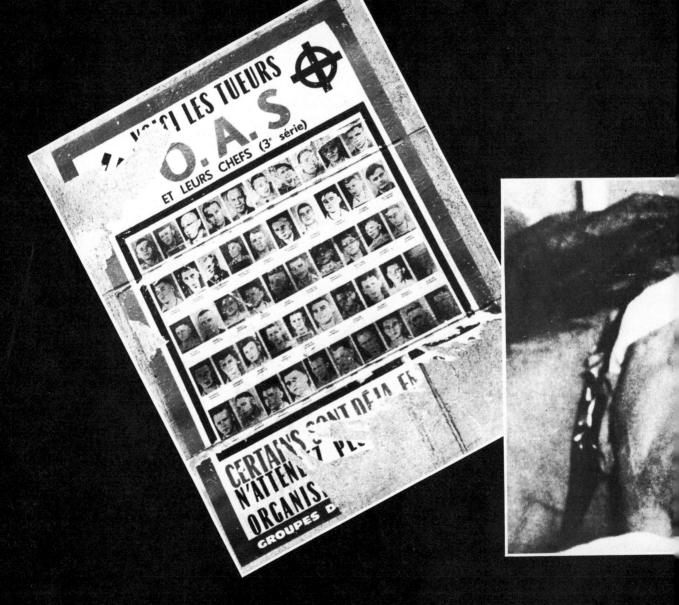

ASSASSINATIONS~
the murders that changed history

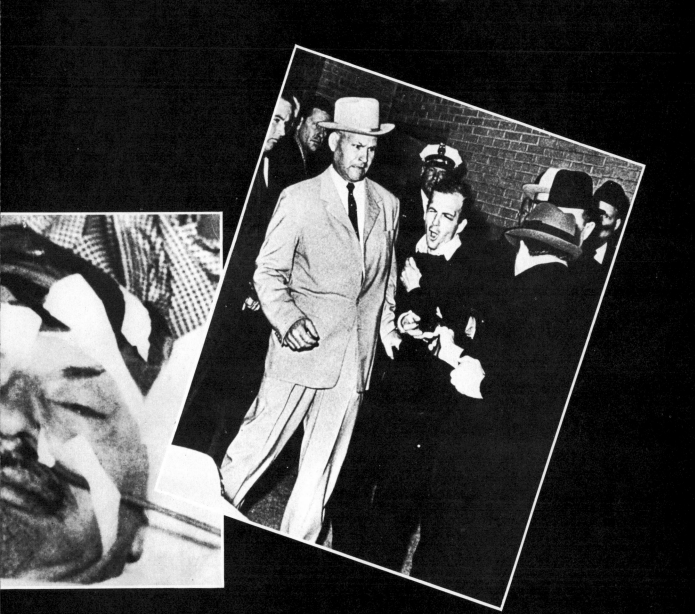

Pictures supplied by:

Front cover: Mansell Collection (top left)
David King (top right)
Mary Evans Picture Library (bottom left)
Keystone Press Agency (bottom centre)
U.S.I.S. (bottom right)
Back cover: Associated Press
Atlantic Press 29 (inset)
Associated Press 105 (bottom)
Biblioteca Imperiale, Teheran 12
Bulloz 14, 16
Camera Press 88 (inset), 107, 119 (inset)
Department of the Environment 68–69, 71
Mary Evans Picture Library 10, 11 (top), 56–57, 70, 92, 99
Historical Picture Service, Chicago 42
Collezione Karmili 4
Keystone Press Agency 24–25, 31 (left and right), 37, 39,
42 (inset), 82, 84 (top), 97, 113
David King 44, 46, 48–49, 50, 53, 54–55
Life Magazine–Time Inc. 100–101
Mansell Collection 18, 40–41, 59 (inset), 64 (bottom), 73,
88–89, 91
National Portrait Gallery, Smithsonian Institution,
Washington D.C. 93
Paris-Match 33
Popperfoto 102 (bottom), 103, 105 (top), 119
Radio Times Hulton Picture Library 22–23, 38 (right),
51, 62, 74, 75, 84 (bottom), 94, 95
Roger-Viollet 26–27, 29, 31 (centre), 38 (left), 76, 78–79,
87
Snark 5, 60
Staatsbibliothek, Berlin 34–35, 81
Sulemaniye Library, Istanbul 11 (bottom)
Sunday Times 56 (inset), 63, 64 (top), 67
Topkapi Palace Museum, Istanbul 9
Transworld Features Inc. 108, 110, 114–115, 116, 117, 120
Photo UNESCO/Documentation Française 20
Castles of the Assassins by P. Willey/George Harrap & Co.
6–7

Published by Marshall Cavendish Publications Limited
58 Old Compton Street
London W1V 5PA

© Marshall Cavendish Publications Limited 1975

Included in this book is extracted material from
Assassination by Brian McConnell published by Leslie
Frewin Publishers Limited © 1969

This volume first published 1975
Printed in Gt. Britain by Ben Johnson & Company Ltd.

ISBN 0 85685 109 4

This edition is not to be sold in the USA,
Canada and the Philippines

CONTENTS

THE OLD MAN OF THE MOUNTAINS

The word 'assassin' comes from the Arabic and was only later adapted in Old French, medieval Latin, Italian and English. Its original form was *hashashin*, the collective name given to the hashish eaters of Persia in the 11th, 12th and 13th centuries. The Crusaders clashed with them and brought back the word in its Old French form, assassin, leaving the Latins to adopt *assassinus*, the Italians *assassino*. The English were content to retain the French form.

The assassins did not, of course, invent murder. They merely gave their name to the kind of murder described. As a group of people they developed out of the schisms in the Muslim faith. Those who believed in the Prophet Mahomet were divided into several sects. They were principally, the orthodox Sunnites, who believed that Mahomet would return to them, and until then should accept the earthly rule of the caliphs, and the unorthodox Shiites or Shiahs, who accepted earthly rule only from the descendants of the Prophet. The unorthodox were, in turn, divided among themselves as to which descendants they should revere. They all agreed on one common collateral descendant, the Prophet's son-in-law, Ali, but after that they divided into four sects over his successors. The two principal factions were the 'twelvers', who supported the succession to the twelfth descendant of Ali, and the 'seveners', who adhered to Ismail, the seventh male descendant. They became the Ismailites.

Penalized and persecuted by the caliphs and the orthodox, they fled from Egypt and settled in Persia. Although unwelcome in the caliphate of

The Castle of Alamut, known as the 'Eagle's Perch', was the home of the original Assassins.

Baghdad, many of them settled and were taught by a series of teachers with their specious sermons until the era of the Father of the Assassins, Hassan Sabbah. His father was a 'twelver', but, forced to profess orthodox views, he sent his son from their hometown of Qumm (now Kum) to Ray (now the ruins of Rhe, near Teheran, capital of Iran) where the Shiites were more welcome. At this point fact and fiction are inseparable.

Castle of the Assassins

Edward Fitzgerald, in his preface to the translation of the *Rubaiyat* of Omar Khayyam, says that the poet went to school with Hassan and Nizam al-Mulk, and tells how they made a pact that whoever succeeded first would help the others. Nizam became a vizier. The poet refused help because he wanted a leisurely life. Hassan was introduced to the court life and given a post, serving the vizier and his Sultan. Judging by their ages, it is more likely that the man who became vizier was their tutor, and that the poet and Hassan were of a similar age. History and fable from there on suggest that Hassan, who had become converted to Ismailism, fell out with the vizier. Either he tried to undermine the vizier's position, or the vizier, seeing in Hassan a rival, trumped up charges against him and had him banished by the Sultan.

In any event, Hassan, like many Ismailites, was an exile and wandered first westwards as far as Cairo, and then eastwards again to the area where he was educated, all the time collecting followers. Eventually he reached the region of Daylam, part of the highlands which frame the southern part of the Caspian Sea. The area had long since been a refuge of the Shiites, independent of the orthodox caliphates. Here 6,000 feet up, on the top of a rock, known locally as 'Eagle's Perch', he found the Castle of Alamut. To reach the castle, in the heart of the Elburz mountains, visitors had to leave the plain of the valley, three miles wide and 30 miles long, and approach the fortification via a narrow, steep and tortuous path rising from the Alamut river. No one could approach surreptitiously. They would be seen approaching. Anyone who reached the path and was unwelcome could be repelled, because the inhabitants looked vertically down on to the narrow path and could block it at will.

Hassan Sabbah decided that this was the place for his kingdom of assassins. The assassins whom he was to lead were to be divided into seven grades of membership. For himself, the chief or sheikh, he chose Sheikh-al-Jebal, literally translated as the Old Man of the Mountains, which instilled respect among his men and terrorized his opponents. After him came the three grand priors, or summoners, with the title Dai-al-Kirbal, and then the Dai's—the missionaries who went out to find recruits for the next lowest, but active rank. The Fida'is, or devoted ones (from the same root as the Fedayeen terrorists of the Middle East in this century), were the actual assassins. Below them came the sixth and seventh orders of the *lasiks*, or masses, who were used for the menial work and knew nothing of the upper echelons of the society.

There was undoubted genius in the organization, and it was shown from the outset in the manner by which Hassan took over the castle. He sent his missionaries in as visitors to the surrounding villages, and then to the castle itself, with the object of converting the inhabitants to Ismailism. Eventually he entered the castle himself, and by the time the Sultan's nominated owner discovered him, there was little the legal resident could do but to accept 3,000 gold pieces in payment for the castle.

The Price of Paradise

The castle was to be the first of many, probably ten or twelve, which would house the assassins. They were recruited from the age of twelve to about twenty and mostly came from the families of peasants who tried to get a living from the barren districts around the mountains. Once inside the castle they could never leave except at the lord-and-master's command. Hassan was a scholar, and he had his recruits taught religion as well as various tongues, including Latin and Greek; but the most important lesson was that of obedience. The reward was paradise.

Exotic chambers and gardens were created at Alamut where the young man was taken to be taught about paradise. Dancing-girls with musical instruments entertained there. The newcomer

ﺳﻴﺪﻧﺎ ﻋﻠﻴﻪ ﻣﺎ ﺍﺳﺘﻰ ﻛﺴﻨﺔ ﻳﻮﺩﻙ ﻗﺘﻞ ﻫﺬﺍ ﺍﻟﺸﻴﻄﺎﻥ ﺍﻭﻝ ﺍﻟﺴﻌﺎﺩﺓ ﺳﺎﻟﻌﻢ ﻭﺍﺯ ﻫﺘﺎﺩ ﻭﺍﺑﺬ ﻛﺪﺳﻨﺘﻪ

Above *An early Persian manuscript records the treacherous and violent slaying of an important enemy of the Order of Assassins.*

would be served with hashish—the tender top and sprout of the hemp plant. Then, waited on by black-eyed *houris*, bathed and scented, the novitiate would be introduced to every sensual pleasure known to mankind. That was paradise. When he was next brought before the Sheikh, he would be assured that he had never left the master's side, but that the master could take him to paradise whenever he wanted. For this, the impressed youth could only repay him in one way—by implicit blind obedience to his word. When the drugged and impressed subject agreed, the Sheikh would give him the word, and the word was: kill. He gave his graduates a golden dagger to do each deed.

When the first ranks of the devoted ones were ready, the Sheikh is supposed to have asked them about his former school colleague, the vizier: 'Who of you will rid the state of the evil Nizam al-Mulk?'

One of the number, Bu Tahir Arrani, taught that the way back to paradise was through such obedience, clasped his right hand across his breast as the sign of acceptance. And on Friday, October 16 1092, or, in the Muslim calendar, the twelfth day of Ramadan in the year 485, the first assassination, in that name, took place. At Nihavand, some 250 miles to the south, Nizam was being taken in a litter from the place where he granted audiences, to the tent of his harem. The devoted one, disguised as a mystic, approached the litter and plunged his golden dagger into the vizier's body. So the hashish eaters, or *hashashin*, gave their names to the assassins.

Rule of Terror

Hassan, in the name of the Ismailites first, for the protection of his own followers second, and for the expansion of their faith, was to dispose of many in this way. 50 assassins and 50 assassinated were listed in his roll-of-honour in the first year at Alamut, and he reigned there for 35 years before dying in 1124. In those years he never left the castle. He devoted his time to reading (he had an excellent library), writing, adding to his religious teaching, and living the life of a monk. He had women but was not licentious; but he abstained from alcohol and certainly from the hashish.

His rule was to use propaganda first, violence second. There never was another alternative because he never failed. It was is if a whole nation was involved in a protection racket. Those who became Ismailites were protected, those who refused were killed. This applied not merely to individuals, but to the inhabitants of castles, villages and towns. If one woman or a whole town rejected the advances of a caliph or his orthodox representatives, then the assassins went to the aid of that woman or that town.

Below *Assassins meet at a street corner to plot the overthrow of their enemies.*

Sovereigns, sultans, princes, generals, caliphs, governors, and even the officials of the mosques, if they were against the believers of Ismail, were slaughtered in this way.

There were numerous attempts to end Hassan's reign and the power of his followers, but he was as adept at espionage and diplomacy as he was at leadership and assassination. More than once, Alamut was put under siege, but each time there was last-minute salvation; a relieving army, a spurious order to the besiegers to withdraw, or other ruses. Hassan's rule was strict. He did not bother to spare two sons. One was assassinated, perhaps wrongfully, for allegedly murdering a prior—a rebellion within the ranks. The other was killed for drinking wine, contrary to the Muslim faith, although it may well have been because this unfortunate toper was seen drinking by one of the uninitiated, making the society's secret vices known.

Not surprisingly, Hassan's own death was rumoured to be via the golden dagger. He had used it, from a distance, often enough. One of his last acts was to bribe a courtier in the Sultan's employ. When the Sultan awoke one morning, after a night's drunken sleep, he found a golden dagger embedded in the floor by his bed. Immediately afterwards, the Sultan received a note from Hassan saying, 'Do I not wish the Sultan well? Otherwise that dagger which was struck into the hard ground would have been planted in his soft breast.' The Sultan, who had refused offers of peace from Hassan (probably very wisely), promptly changed his mind.

Dynasty of Death

Hassan's successor at Alamut was his brother-in-law, Buzurgumid, who for twenty years had commanded the assassins' second castle at Lammasar. The new Sheikh was more of an administrator than an intriguer, but his assassins carried on the same bloody work with the same ideals. In fourteen years he accounted for a caliph, two prefects, and a *mufti*, plus many other prominent figures, and when two of his priors, acting as ambassadors to the Sultan, were lynched by a mob, the assassins attacked the town of Qazvin, killed an emir, 400 people, and captured a considerable quantity of riches.

Muhammed, the next Sheikh, who ruled for

Above *Remote and aloof, the Old Man of the Mountains instructs his followers.*

Below right *The Old Man of the Mountains at work with his scribes. Despite his violent deeds the despot was a fine scholar.*

24 years until 1162, found opposition in his son, Hassan. The son was a scholar, while his father was not. When the people began to listen more to his son, he punished them by killing 250 of them and tying their lifeless bodies onto the backs of 250 others who had been condemned, driving them away from the castle. When Muhammed died, the 35-year-old son, Hassan, succeeded. It is thought that the father tried to poison the son, but Hassan put the noxious substance in his father's cup first.

Beginning of the End

The new ruler, to bind the assassins more closely to him, abandoned some of the tenets of the Muslim faith. While his predecessors had preached that they must wait for the Imam, or teacher, to arrive on earth, Hassan, in the middle of a fast, had a pulpit built facing away from Mecca, and preached that he had had a message from the Imam and that he was his chosen one. Wearing white robes, and a white turban, he mounted the pulpit, held aloft his sword and addressed 'the worlds, *jinn*, men, and angels', and pronounced that he could 'free you

from the burden of the rules of Holy Law, and has brought you to the Resurrection'. Music was played and the Sheikh openly swigged wine in the pulpit while blasphemously facing away from Mecca.

He was so powerful that many of his followers believed in him, and he ordered that those who did not abandon the Holy Law, from which he had freed them, be chastised and stoned to death. This was obviously blasphemy and sacrilege. His brother-in-law appointed himself an assassin and stabbed Hassan to death. Hassan was succeeded by Mahomet II and, after an uneventful reign, was poisoned by his son Jalal-al-Din, in 1220. The new Sheikh abandoned Ismailism and sought the allegiance of the Sultan and caliphs by promising to bring his supporters back into the orthodox fold of Islam. Various truces were made, but Ismailism survived—and so did assassination. Even when Jalal-al-Din died, the assassins were still there to do the bidding of his son, Alaeddin Mahomet III, crippled and mentally deranged. He was made successor to the Old Man of the Mountains at the age of nine, and ruled as a puppet until the conflict between him and his son, Rukn al-Din Khurshah,

came to a head in 1225. One night while the son lay ill in bed and apparently incapacitated, an assassin plunged the golden dagger into the breast of his father. The reign of the assassins, in Persia at least, was coming to an end. Genghis Khan and his long-haired Mongol horseman had crossed Asia and were now in Muslim lands. They had already taken Samarkand and invaded Georgia, Armenia and Mesopotamia. Now they were in Iran, carrying orders to subdue all lands until they reached Egypt. What could the assassins do against the Golden Horde? Genghis Khan had sent his grandson, the Mongol prince Helegu, to complete this task, and while the Sultan and caliphs submitted to him, and were massacred, the last Old Man of the Mountains tried to hold out. After all, the Ismaili castles were formidable fortresses. They had withstood many attacks and could be useful, and that is why they attracted the special attention of Hulegu.

Legacy of Murder

Rukn al-Din could not make up his mind. He sent emissaries to the Mongols, but they were rejected. He sent gifts to Hulegu and they were accepted. But Helegu wanted the castles. The assassins' leader made the long journey to the Mongol capital of Karakorum, but Genghis Khan refused to see him and sent him away with the message that, if he dismantled and surrendered the castles, he might then be permitted to prostrate himself before his Mongol superiors.

Rukn al-Din had prevaricated long enough. As he made his way back to Persia, he and his entourage were offered hospitality at a feast away from the travellers' route. There the assassins were themselves assassinated. As one Persian historian put it: 'He and his followers were put to the sword; and of him and his stock no trace was left, and he and his kindred became but a tale on men's lips and a tradition in thè world.' Poetic, but not quite true, for part of the vast following of Ismail had long

Left *A Mongol army captures an Assassin's castle; against Genghis Khan's hordes the Order had no defence.*

since left Persia and settled in Syria. They continued their activities, particularly in the time of the Crusades. They had had a period of consolidation, but when the Crusaders under the banner of the Cross went to recover possession of the Holy Land from the Saracens, they found the new enemy. At the gates of Bahram, they murdered Count Raymond II of Tripoli, their first Frankish victim, and later they struck down Conrad of Montserrat, king of the Latin Kingdom of Jerusalem. This was a great coup, for the assassins, disguised as Christian monks, had managed to ingratiate themselves into the presence of the king, his bishop and other nobles, before striking them down with their daggers.

When captured, the assassins were well briefed in the stories they had to tell. To Conrad's men, they told how they had been sent by King Richard Coeur de Lion to kill their master. (Curiously Conrad's widow was soon married to one of Richard's allies and protégés, Count Henry of Champagne, who then became Conrad's successor!) But the assassins' own stories could scarcely match those told about them. They and their opponents were perhaps the original cowboys and indians, the first blood-and-thunder adversaries. They were powerful, strengthened an important sect of the Muslim creed, but despite their many successes they could never become a national or international force. They held castles and small towns and were forever a threat to law-and-order, but as assassins they did not survive the Middle Ages. Storytellers have seized on isolated instances of banditry, violence and murder to revive them, but the descendants are merely Ismaili faithful— small people tilling the soil, selling goods.

There are said to be some 50,000 of them left in the world today, and for the last 150 years their hereditary leader has had the title of His Highness the Aga Khan.

The murderous traits of his people have long since gone, but they left that name, assassin, for thousands more to follow. In the following pages many are dealt with. The list is endless. This volume may not be the last, definitive work on assassination, but it is designed to show why assassination, proven or not, seldom if ever justified, carried out by worthy or worthless people on their worthy or worthless fellows, is a compelling subject of study in the history of crime.

MARAT~ BLOODY REVOLUTIONARY

The French, with their penchant for adding to the usual interpretations of life, love, art and crime, can be expected to have redefined such a cardinal act as assassination. Their record of sudden, public murder extended over centuries has offered some notable examples, with artistic touches, and, in the case of one recent French leader, a certain fixation in their attempts. (They have a national tendency to cry 'assassin' at the slightest pretext, at politicians, art critics and foreign cooks.) They may be excused for using the word assassination for some murders which do not fit the accepted definition of the word, since they have achieved some and attempted others which are classic cases of the world's most shocking crime.

But, in the whole history of France, the subject of assassination must principally refer to two men who led France nearly 170 years apart. Both were much hated men, perhaps, to some of their sub-jects, the most hated in history, the most reviled of all time. They are fascinating subjects because of the measure of hatred that they have been capable of engendering, inviting and suffering during their lives—sufficient to make them prime targets for assassination.

Doctor and Revolutionary

Jean Paul Marat, as he was born, was by nature belligerently independent. He was the son of a doctor, who had himself abandoned his national

Marat in death. David's famous painting is a romanticized view of a man who, when in power, had the blood of hundreds on his hands.

religion to marry a Swiss protestant woman. Jean left his home, on the death of his mother, to study medicine and to travel. He was sixteen years of age, studied medicine at Bordeaux, then went on to Paris, where he made use of his knowledge of optics and electricity to subdue an obstinate disease of the eyes. From Paris he went to Holland and then settled in Church Street, Soho, at that time a fashionable London street, where his medical doctorate appeared on his nameplate, a doctorate which, incidentally, he received from St. Andrews University.

At the age of 30 he had published an opinionated *Philosophical Essay on Man*, in two volumes, in which he described an attempt to investigate the principles and laws of the reciprocal influence of the soul on the body; the third volume was not completed. Although he published a political pamphlet, *The Chains of Slavery*, in 1774, he chose to remain anonymous. It was circulated in constituencies where the electors who read it may have been encouraged to return popular representatives rather than friends of the King, but either its cost or small circulation, or its arguments, did not influence the election of that year. The reason Marat may have kept his name off the pamphlet was his own growing influence with the aristocracy, Charles X having appointed him physician to his guards at 2,000 livres per year plus allowances.

His forays into the literary-medico, literary-scientific and literary-philosophical fields brought

Marat in life. From an obscure career as a doctor, Marat rose to power in the Revolution and became one of the chief architects of the 'Terror' which swept across France.

him criticism, because he dared to attack such names as Helvétius the once highly thought of philosopher, and to contradict such authorities as Sir Isaac Newton. This led him to being rejected by the *Académie des Sciences*, but he found support for his criticism of his fellow countrymen among a group which included Benjamin Franklin and Goethe. Even Brissot, who was later to be one of his most violent opponents, advanced the view that Marat had considerable scientific influence, particularly in the field of heat, light and electricity.

Certainly Marat's ability as a doctor, reputation as a scientist, and his conversation as a philosopher, earned him admission into some of the stately homes as well as the Court of Paris; but all that was soon to end. The Revolution was on the way. The crops of 1788 had failed in a summer hailstorm. The Exchequer was bankrupt and the financial administration suspect. The people tied to the land could only flee to the city, and into the melting-pot of Parisian discontent came all the masses. To cool the malcontents, Louis XVI, despite the interference of his Queen, Marie Antoinette, recalled the Estates General.

Bid for Power

When that body, comprising the three estates, clergy, nobility and anti-privilege group, failed to agree, revolution was imminent. Abbé Siéyès, who wrote that 'the third Estate is the nation, less the privileged orders', was joined by Marat who produced similar views in *Offrande à la Patrie*. It was at this time that Marat emerged in the public eye.

The third estate, joined by some of the clergy sought to call themselves the National Assembly, and among them was a powerful group of Anglomaniacs who believed that the best policy was to adopt the British 'constitution', that is to say that those methods of governing Britain, which were understood and accepted, should be written into a French constitution. Marat had admittedly lived in England, but he began to show extreme views to assert his knowledge and authority, first in a report, *Tableau des Vices de la Constitution d'Angleterre*. This he presented to the Assembly and said that England was really in the hands of royalty, an

example which France should not follow. The argument was adjourned but Marat was perpetually there, the lone man, the lone voice, seeking the lone power.

When soldiers fired on the people, there arose a new civil guard, the Parisian militia, who on July 14 1789 seized the arms at Les Invalides and then, in the spirit of civil war, stormed the Bastille prison, the outworn ancient symbol of despotic monarchy, and razed it to the ground.

To Britons, Americans, or any of the other democracies, the constitution demanded by the representatives of the French people was of fundamental principles. The *Declaration des Droits de l'Homme* was somewhat highflown a description for the humanity it sought, and the seventeen points embodied in it should have raised no eyebrows among people conversant with the English Bill of Rights and the American Declaration. But this was France, and the demands of the constitution produced a resistance from the nobility, and an exaggerated demand for its extension from Marat. From his pinnacle of loneliness he shouted down at the people, not only with his voice, but with his newspapers, first the *Moniteur Patriote*, then *Publiciste Parisien* and finally under its best-known title *L'Ami du Peuple*. Its message, in a word, was: denounce.

In Exile

Marat, the man without a close political colleague, without a party, saw opposition in everything. No man ever really meant what he said. No party ever fully represented what it set out to represent. Poverty should never be accepted. Misery should never be overlooked. Persecution had only one benefit—the discovery of traitors to the cause of the Revolution. Discover, denounce and pursue were the actions he proposed to the Assembly and continually advocated in his columns. Denounce an enemy and that person would be hounded by *L'Ami du Peuple* until found innocent or guilty. Its publisher had his own cry: '*Nous sommes trahis*'.

He did not have to be betrayed. His opposition to the powerful, though more moderate, elements of the Republic forced him to flee to London.

When he returned he had to join the other people in hiding in the cellars and sewers of Paris. It was there that he contracted a skin disease of a scrofulous nature which was to waste away the frame of the man. The Constituent Assembly, having produced the simple constitution, dissolved itself and opened the way for the new Legislative Assembly, which was to have the job of operating the constitution, and governing the First Republic. Its members, mostly belonging to parties, consisted of the right and extreme right—the origin of the position of political parties—as they took their seats on that side of the President's chair, and the left and extreme left. These were, respectively, the *Feuillants,* or constitutionalists, to the right. To the left were the *Girondists,* who originated from Bordeaux, who supported the constitution, and, because of their educational background, were an attractive, eloquent and patriotic group. Representing the small trader class they had sympathies with extreme republicans but could not bring themselves to join forces with the extreme left, or, as it was known, 'The Mountain'. This group was composed of the popular delegates, and the representatives of the *Jacobins* and the *Cordeliers* clubs.

There sat Robespierre, Danton, and Camille Desmoulins. It was Danton of the *Cordeliers* club who recalled Marat, the man who would sit by himself, to help the new Republic. He disagreed with everybody but became so revolutionary that none could supplant him without the fear of being denounced. Robespierre was the ascetic, who lived, worked and slept in surroundings of bare discomfort because he was the soul of the Revolution, and his austerity brought the poor and the hungry to worship him. Danton, more moderate, had seen the Republic arrive through revolution and wanted the spirit of the insurrectionists to be dampened down now for the good of the country. Marat suspected everybody in authority, and the numerical majority of people who agreed were the *Girondists.*

Reign of Terror

Meanwhile the Court of Louis XVI had gone over to the *émigrés* who had quit France at the first shouts of republicanism. No one would leave the Assembly for the frontiers of Austria when Paris might fall into the hands of enemies of the Republic. With the Duke of Brunswick on the march to Paris, and Paris vacillating between going to meet him, and

Above *The revolutionary mob storms the Bastille – symbol of the royalist oppression.*

Right *An aristocrat is carried to execution – another victim for Madame Guillotine.*

suspicious that the King was the traitor who had invited the enemy, the Republic was in danger. It was left to the *Jacobins* to start an insurrection within an insurrection and to take charge. This group, which took its name from a *Jacobin* convent meeting-place, had soldiers, who gave their name to the *Marseillaise,* later the national anthem, took the Tuileries and the Hôtel de Ville, massacred the guard, and made way for the new government of Robespierre and Danton.

The King had sought the protection of the old Assembly, while his Swiss guards, whom he had employed because he could not trust French ones, were annihilated. The King was held prisoner at the Luxembourg, the rest of the royal family at the Temple. And, from that day of August 10 1792, the reign of terror had begun. The prisons were filled, executioners were hired at six francs per day, the mockery of trials were set up, and the new Paris Commune entered into the era of the bloodbath.

Robespierre thought that Providence had intended him to be dictator of the commonwealth. Danton, the advocate, was too much of an advocate to seize any chance for power, and he was content to serve. But it was Marat, the man without party, who demanded the committee of surveillance, the office of suspicion, the means by which he and he alone would purify society. Only he knew and only he could decide who was pure. And to ensure that this was done he took his seat in the new Assembly. He closed his newspaper, *L'Ami du Peuple,* and replaced it with another, the *Journale de la République Française,* a more respectable title, perhaps, but which published the same sentiments as before: suspect, denounce and keep watching for the enemies of the republic.

In the new Assembly, the *Girondists* had moved to the right, still with an actual majority, while on the left were the *Jacobins,* known as 'The Mountain' and below them the groups who, according to their more moderate views, were known as the 'plain' and the 'marsh'. While the *Girondists* had their support in the country, notably Bordeaux, Normandy and other far-off places, the powerful left came from Paris, which had returned 24 deputies. Marat was the seventh of them.

Extremely unpopular, he demanded a tribunal to try royalists in prison, to show the people what would happen to them; but no tribunal was set up and the prison massacres of August and September took place. While Paris was still threatened by war, the city took its principal revenge with the trial of King Louis XVI. His title no longer existed so he was tried under the name Louis Capet, and eventually, on a vote of 387–334, he was sentenced to death. Again it was Marat who insisted that there should be a trial, that the King should be properly represented, but for the good of the people, he must go to the guillotine.

Counter~Revolution

With all the Royalists in prison, guillotined or on their way to execution, the revolutionaries could concentrate on their other formidable opponents, the *Girondists*. This numerically strong party hated Danton and accused him of being responsible for the September massacres, although Danton had in fact, after accepting popular passion and bloodshed as inevitable in revolution, tried to find a compromise between the *Girondists* and the *Jacobins*. While the *Girondists* spent their time and energy attacking the other parties, Marat conducted a relentless struggle against these moderate constitutionalists. They hated Marat because he belonged to bloody republicanism. Marat hated them because they had ridden on the bandwagon of republicanism, had suffered nothing and now sought to rule.

The Convention which replaced the Assembly set up a Committee of Twelve, composed of *Girondists*. The Paris deputies ordered the Committee to be disbanded, and decided to set up themselves a Committee of Public Safety. The Convention had ordered that Marat should be tried by the *Tribunal Revolutionnaire*, but Marat was acquitted and he returned to public life just as the Paris deputies suppressed the Committee of Twelve. Marat, at the head of the *sans-culottes*, the only 'party' he ever knew, overthrew the *Girondists*, arrested two ministers and 31 deputies. The result was that more than half the 83 departments of France rose to defend the banned party. *Emigrés* returned from abroad when they heard that the Republic had split, while the new Central Revolutionary Committee could only claim a few departments around Paris. There was no one strong enough to attack the Paris of Robespierre and Danton and Marat.

Marat was now 50 and a sick man, and had to spend much of his life in warm baths to combat the skin disease he had contracted in the subterranean hiding places of Paris. It was in this position that he frequently sat and wrote articles for the *Journale* denouncing the *Girondists* whom he hated. Now, at last, they were beaten, except for small groups of them, one in Normandy.

An Unlikely Assassin

It was at Caen in Normandy that Charlotte Corday first heard of the *Girondists*. Marie-Anne-Charlotte Corday D'Armont, born at St Saturnin, near Séez in Normandy, had been educated at a convent, at the expense of her well-to-do parents, and had then gone to live with an aunt at Caen. Here she passed most of her time reading classics, such as Plutarch and Voltaire. When the *Girondists* fell she heard that their leaders were setting up headquarters in Normandy, and there she heard Jeanne Pierre Brissot, who used the name de Warville; he denounced Marat at a public meeting. He told his supporters: 'You will find your reward in helping France beneath the blade of the guillotine. This monster is unfeeling, violent and cruel. Three hundred thousand heads must be struck off before liberty is established. That will be until this man Marat, whose soul is kneaded in blood and dirt, and is a disgrace to humanity and to the revolution, is dead.'

Mme Corday was already thinking of going to Paris. She had obtained the necessary passport in April for her journey before the fall of the *Girondists*, but now her mission became important. She was to go in July, a girl of 24 years, just five feet-one inch tall, with auburn hair and grey eyes. She had a prominent forehead, and long nose, but the mouth was average and the chin prettily dimpled in her oval face. This, then, was the convent-educated young woman, who had been sheltered by her aunt from the French world of revolution, who went alone to Paris in July of 1793. She attended to some business for a friend in Caen and then wrote to Marat:

'*Citoyen,* I have just arrived from Caen. Your love for your native place doubtless makes you desirous of learning the events which have occurred in that part of the republic.' In this she was mistaken. Marat was born at Neuchâtel on the Swiss–French frontier. Nevertheless her letter continued, 'I shall call at your residence in about an

Left *Charlotte Corday. Was she motivated by a personal hatred of Marat, or was she the willing agent of a group, such as the Girondists, who had suffered at the hands of Marat?*

hour. Have the goodness to receive me and grant me a brief interview. I will put you in a condition to render a great service to France.'

The Fatal Meeting

When she called within an hour she was refused admission, so she wrote again, promising to reveal important secrets, and appealing to Marat as a revolutionary leader of the Republic to help her, who had been persecuted by the enemies of the Republic. Having despatched that note she called again and was again refused admission, but on her third visit Marat, hearing voices raised in the ante-room, agreed to see her while he remained in his medicinal bath. No one knows for certain to this day whether she acted as a patriot, on one or a few incitements by *Girondist* propaganda, or whether she knew someone in the movement in Caen who had sent her to deal with Marat.

In any event, she was shown into his presence, and while he sat in his bath, wrapped in towels, his diseased and decaying flesh in an advanced form of putrefaction, she told him of the *Girondists* in Normandy. She gave him names, and he wrote them down before telling her, 'I will have them all guillotined at Paris.' At this she pulled from her bosom a table-knife which she had bought for two francs the previous day, and plunged it into Marat's body, piercing the lung and severing the aorta. All that Marat could do was to cry, '*A moi, ma chère amie*'. This brought to the room two women servants, one of whom was Simonne Evrard, the woman who had remained faithful to him through the years, and the only one who helped dress his diseased body.

The two women held Charlotte Corday until guards came for her and took her to the prison of the Abbaye. Charged before the Revolutionary Tribunal, she mocked her accusers, and when the indictment was read and she was asked if she wished to say anything, Mme Corday replied, with dignity, 'Nothing, except that I have succeeded.' Her advocate pleaded that she was insane, but she insisted that her only defence was her avowal of her act of assassination. 'That is the only defence worthy of me,' she added.

Sentenced to death, she was taken to the *Conciergerie,* where she commissioned Hauer, the portraitist, to paint her likeness, which is today in the Versailles Museum. From there she wrote to Caen, and recalling her readings of Roman literature: she said, 'I long to be with Brutus in Elysian fields.' With this anticipation of happiness she wrote a tender farewell to her father. Then on July 17, just two days afterwards, *l'ange de l'assassinat,* as she was called, was taken to the guillotine. She gave an involuntary but momentary shudder when she saw the contraption, but then knelt and put her head in position without assistance from anyone and the knife fell, but not before she had uttered her last words: 'I have a right to be curious. I have never seen one before.'

The executioner picked up her severed head and struck it with his other fist to the cheers of the mob. After all, he owed his post largely to Jean Paul Marat.

An enraged mob confronts the assassin. In fact Marat's death was a timely event; post-revolutionary France was sick of the blood-bath which he had instigated.

DE GAULLE~ TARGET OF THE OAS

For those who shudder at the thought of murder—and particularly assassination—and the horror of death and assassination at the time of the French Revolution, consider what would be required in the way of duty, hatred, honour, or revenge to commit assassination in the 20th century. There has been bloodshed in this century, but no bloodbath of the Parisian proportions. There has been a silent revolution in France over its colonial empire, but not a revolution of the order of the late 18th century. What then happened to General Charles de Gaulle, President of France from 1958 to 1969? Who would want to kill him and why? The answers

lie as much in the origins of de Gaulle's rise to fame and power as in the immediate happenings before the attempts to end his life.

Before World War One, de Gaulle had only just reached senior rank in the Army, that is the rank of a two-star general, and although he had written one book and some treatises on military strategy, he was not regarded as a leading military commander. When, in 1940, he saw the politicians who had refused to listen to him in the 'thirties capitulating to the German armies, he escaped to Britain, but not in the spirit of someone whose country has been overrun and who must now seek sanctuary with a

Autocratic, overbearing, haughty – Charles de Gaulle in a typical pose.

friendly power. De Gaulle's attitude, and there were sufficient hints, allusions and references to it, was that Britain owed France, and particularly the French Army, a great deal. He liked to remind Britain, as Marshal Pétain had reminded Mr Churchill, that she should have gone to the aid of French armies in World War One, and, on his own, he thought that she should have done more in the defence of the Maginot line between September 1939 and the spring of 1940 when the Nazis smashed through it.

From then on, for more than a quarter of a century, he was to be a difficult ally to Britain, a formidable opponent to his own countrymen who opposed him, and a very likely target for assassination. His physical features made him always easily identifiable, and his prominent profile, his six-feet-four-inches from which he towered over most crowds, his habit of leaving escorts and guards to talk and shake hands with likely supporters, made him a difficult person to guard effectively. Yet his escapes were phenomenal.

An Uneasy Alliance

In the early days of World War Two it seemed doubtful if he would survive in any senior Free French capacity whatsoever. He sought sole superior command over many other senior generals who were prepared to fight with the Allies, not the least of whom was General Giraud, in command in North Africa. A not inconsiderable piece of diplomatic war effort had to be made by Harold Macmillan, then British Minister Resident in North Africa, in keeping Britain's allies together, due to the temperamental and personal animosities among those allies. While General de Gaulle wanted complete command of all anti-German French troops all over the world, he was unwilling to recognize, help or promote the activities of the French underground movement. From his headquarters in Britain he ordered M. Georges Bidault, who was later to become a member of his peace-time government, that the assassination of Germans occupying France was to cease because of the reprisals such action might bring on the innocent civilian population. He also promoted the idea at the

end of World War Two that there had been no French underground, that the *Maquis* was largely ideological, and that there had been only one saviour of France and that was General de Gaulle's Free French services.

It is no wonder that Mr Churchill, after many grievances towards de Gaulle and complaints of his behaviour, looked at the Free French emblem and said, 'The most difficult Cross I have ever had to bear is that of Lorraine.'

Power Struggle for France

During the war, many people had suggested and said publicly that France would never emerge again as a great power. General de Gaulle of France was determined that she would so succeed and with him at the head. Even at the victory celebrations in Paris in 1945, he showed that he intended to command. Even though he towered over those around him he waved with both arms to the joyful crowds and, as M. Bidault recalled to the author later, 'The General imperceptibly steered me from his right to the left, so that few noticed it, but everyone was aware of who was in the centre—the General.' It was on this walk to the famous Cathedral of Nôtre Dame that from a height, from somewhere near the Rose window, or from the belfry of the hunchback, a single sniper's shot rang out to warn de Gaulle of the danger of assassination. Whoever it was, and it is thought to have been a Communist member of the underground movement (which de Gaulle insisted did not exist), he missed.

After the tedious succession of governments,

cabinets and prime minsters which followed the war, the General, with or without the de Gaullist party he had formed about him, was still the only conceivable head of France. Imperious, arrogant, and contemptuous of other nations and peoples, he built around him a legend of invincibility. He attracted the type of humour which fits such situations. Did he say *'Je suis France'*? He is credited with some of the best apocryphal stories of his time. He is supposed to have denied the immortality of Paris, and said it was a misunderstanding for his own immortality. *'Après moi le déluge'* is attributed to him, just as it was de Gaulle and not the Emperor Tiberius who said, 'When I am dead, let fire destroy the earth.'

A man with de Gaulle's authority must have enemies, but the General, through his policies of autocratic rule, based on his own beliefs, his own arguments, his own conclusions, and his own

decisions, brought him near to death on many occasions. The most numerous of them occurred after he introduced his policy of decolonising the French empire. After France's failure to keep the Communists out of Indo-China, and the terrible defeat of her forces at Dien Bien Phu, de Gaulle turned his attention to granting independence to French Algeria.

Algeria~the Flashpoint

Algeria had been French since May 1830, when Admiral Duperre sailed from Toulon with General Bourmont in charge of 37,000 infantrymen and 4,000 cavalry, to take over the territory which had been fought over by the Romans, and every major power in that area since. Now, in 1960, that sphere of French influence was to end. De Gaulle was willing to surrender Algeria in the wake of terrible bloodshed there from the Fronte Liberation Nationale (FLN). He could go to the people and they would agree with him that Algeria should have independence. The people he could not persuade, even

Surrounded by vigilant Secret Service men, Le General and his motorcade of VIPs celebrate the anniversary of the Liberation of France.

if he really wanted to try, were those upon whom he had relied during the war and after the war—his colleagues, M. Jacques Soustelle and M. Georges Bidault, Generals Raoul Salan and Edouard Jouhaud, ex-General Paul Gardy and Colonel Antoine Argoud. Most of them had never heard of their leader before 1940 when he arrived in London; after 1960 they hoped they would never hear of him again.

Soustelle, who had been the architect of political Gaullism, quit the General's movement. He told his President and former colleague: 'If you surrender Algeria to the fanatical and terrorist sect you will open the way for rivers of blood to flow through that country'. To which the President replied, 'You cannot build a policy on fears.' He then dismissed Soustelle. Bidault had been in charge of the French underground, was a former Prime Minister, a former Foreign Minister, and now a rebel. De Gaulle dismissed him, despite his loyal services to France.

A President may do without his political colleagues. There will always be a queue of replacements no matter what the policy. But what about the Army? Not only in metropolitan France were senior army officers either quitting the service or openly rebelling, but in Algeria itself the famous parachute regiment, *les paras,* were now against the policy of surrender. The First Foreign Legion Parachute Regiment was in the forefront of the opposition. With it, Generals Maurice Challe, André Zelle, Raoul Salan and Edouard Jouhaud wielded considerable military influence. Colonels like Antoine Argoud and officers of similar and lesser rank could be counted on to operate any plan of revolt. Former Prime Minister M. Georges Bidault and former government minister Jacques Soustelle could be relied upon to give the revolt political justification.

The Secret Armies

The military rebels first formed the *Organisation de l'Armée Secrete* (OAS), while the civil and political objectors had formed the Council of National Resistance (CNR). Acting at times separately and then together, as if completely merged and integrated, some had only one definition of revolt—the

assassination of President Charles de Gaulle. They were to try to kill him six times, at a conservative estimate, although the French Secret Service has good evidence to suggest that the total number of attempts on the General's life reached a double figure proportion. So high was he on the list of targets for possible assassination that bookmakers quoted odds of twenty-to-one against such an incident, and the insurance giants of the City of London refused to underwrite his life for the benefit of disinterested third-party writers, commentators and film-makers.

In 1961, after seven years bitter fighting in Algeria, between nationalists who chose terrorism to attack the French authorities and the authorities who would use torture to put down the terrorists, the General sought the popular vote to hand over Algeria to an independent government. He received support of some 75% although there were considerable abstentions. He also faced two years of attempts on his life.

The granting of independence to Algeria, an inevitable result of the 'winds of change' which Mr Macmillan had seen blowing across the African continent, was bound to provoke opposition from certain vested interests like those of businessmen and farmers who had been in Algeria all their lives, like their fathers before them. Likewise, the Army had a vested interest, since the ending of French rule in North Africa would mean the end of the French Foreign Legion—there would be a legion with no foreign territories to police. But in addition to these factors there was the terrible massacre of 80 Europeans in the Rue d'Isly of Algiers in March 1961, after the Franco-Algerian cease-fire. As they marched in a much larger body to protest against the French policy in Algeria, Muslim and French troops opened fire on the demonstrators, causing this terrible death-roll. Although the authorities claimed that their troops had been fired on first, the rebels had already named the person they believed to be the culprit—General de Gaulle.

"A Joke in Bad Taste"

Within two months of that massacre, he was driving from Paris to his home at Colombey-les-Deux Eglises when a bomb exploded near his car. In May

Above *A shop and hotel bombed by members of the OAS. Increasingly, the secret army carried its war to the streets of France.*

Inset *A soldier in the Parachute Regiment – backbone of the OAS – is led away to arrest.*

of the following year, while touring central France, police discovered a plot for a sniper to assassinate the President as he walked into Mass. Within six months of that massacre he was driving from his estate at Colombey, 120 miles south-east of Paris, when an explosion rocked his car. At Pont-sur-Seine, Aube, 80 lbs of plastic bomb had been buried in sand on the edge of the road, to be detonated by the vibration of the cars in his convoy —a chancy method which did not succeed in damaging any of the cars or in injuring any of the party. The General dismissed it as a joke 'in very bad taste', a joke which cost the perpetrators prison sentences of twenty years for one of their number, fifteen years for three of them, and ten years for a fifth.

On another occasion the General, on a provincial tour, was warned by leaflets not to go to Mass at Poitiers Cathedral, in the centre of France, because he had the blood of martyrs on his hands. The leaflets were signed dramatically, Charles Martel, the name of the man who defeated the Saracens at Poitiers in 732: and attempts were made to dissuade the Archbishop from receiving the President at the steps of the Cathedral, in case, it was suggested, he might also be harmed.

But the biggest attempt on the life of the General, the best organized, planned in every detail, by a hand-picked team of fifteen assassins, was to come at approximately 8 pm on the night of August 22 1962.

Ambush

At 7.45 pm, at the side-entrance of the Elysée Palace, police-driver Henri Marroux opened the doors of the official presidential Citroën to help the President and Madame de Gaulle to occupy the rear seats. Into the front passenger seat clambered their son-in-law, Colonel Alain de Boisseau, who acted as the General's adjutant. They were heading for the airport at Villacoublay, from where the three passengers were to fly by Air Force plane to St Dizier.

They were already behind schedule, and as the second identical black Citroën, full of secret-service men, drove across the road from the Sûreté headquarters to join the small motorcade, four police motor-cycle engines were revved up to start the fast and nearly fatal drive. The route to be taken would be the Route Nationale 306 via the Paris suburb of Petit-Clamart.

There, the assassins waited. Lieutenant-Colonel Jean-Marie Bastien-Thiry, acting on the plan of the others, waited by a bus-stop facing Paris and the convoy. When he sighted the first riders, he was to signal with a rolled copy of *France-Soir* which he held in his hand so that a machine-gunner, hidden behind a parked van on the opposite side of the road, could open fire when the procession was a mere 150 yards away. What was to happen next was a classical ambush as taught at the *École de Guerre*. While the machine-gunner burst the tyres of the oncoming vehicles from their right, a car, parked in a turning to the left of them, would decimate the entourage by cross-fire. There would be no chance of escape.

So meticulous were the would-be assassins that at a late stage they decided to augment their murderous force. Four men would be used to slow and halt the presidential car, two with 9 mm machine-pistols and two with automatic rifles. That should stop the principal target in the road, while the marksmen in the second car would cut off the escape and from close quarters assassinate the President. At such close range they could hardly miss. In addition to the marksmen's military training, they had practised shooting so that at 300 yards they could put all their bullets within a five-inch circle. Since the shots in this operation would all be well within 150 yards, nothing could presumably go wrong. They could not fail.

Bastien-Thiry saw the motorcade approach and waved his newspaper downwards—and the plot failed. The first marksman, seeing the cars and motor-cycles approach, hesitated. As they were travelling at 60 miles per hour, that hesitation meant that when he did fire they were nearer 50 yards away and too near to be stopped effectively. As bullets hit the tyres, de Boisseau, the adjutant, shouted to his father- and mother-in-law to get down, and to the driver to accelerate. Although the tyres were hit and he first went into a violent skid, he corrected the car and drove on. The assassins' second car pulled out of the side-turning, its driver not understanding the delay in opening fire; he drove out between the President's car and the rear motor-cycle escort; de Gaulle

Above *De Gaulle waged an unceasing campaign against the OAS. Georges Watin,* **Left,** *one of the marksmen who attempted to assassinate de Gaulle at Petit-Clamart, eluded the police dragnet; but Lt-Colonel Jean Bastien-Thiry,* **Right,** *paid with his life for his part in the plot. Anti OAS propaganda,* **Centre,** *and the use of double agents helped smash the OAS.*

could still die.

From the front passenger seat, on the right of the driver, Georges Watin went into action. An Algerian-born engineer and farm-owner and now an OAS agent, he leaned out of the car and fired rapidly at the Venetian-blind-covered rear window of the presidential vehicle. Ten shots shattered that window before the driver could get the car out of range, ten shots skimming inches above the hidden heads of the President and his wife,

miraculously missing both the driver and the adjutant, too. When the presidential car reached the next major intersection the OAS pursuers were forced to abandon their pursuit. Unfortunately, when the *gendarmerie* of Petit-Clamart, informed that an attempt had been made on the President's life, arrived on the scene the only clues available to them were 150 spent cartridge cases. Even an abandoned car, found within a kilometre's distance, left them with virtually untraceable clues. The car had been stolen, the two automatic rifles, five magazines, a kilogram of plastic explosive, two smoke-bombs and a phosphorus grenade missile were army property. With so many military rebels, who could say who stole what? And from where?

The General reached Villacoublay and said grimly, 'That was a close shave.' He looked at his watch, dusted glass from his coat and added, 'We are fifteen minutes late.'

Nationwide Hunt

Assassins are too often dismissed as cranks, nobodies, madmen and lunatics, but the French

Government had no illusions about this attempt. The OAS had openly boasted that de Gaulle would be assassinated, and behind the OAS were distinguished politicans and military experts. They would not have fired the guns, of course, and therefore it would be exceptionally difficult to accuse them under ordinary laws. Their devotees who did fire the guns would be extremely difficult to discover and identify.

It was here that the police received information by luck so often necessary to a successful investigation. More than 360 miles away, near Valence on the Route Nationale 7 between Lyons and the gateways to the Mediterranean coast, *gendarmes,* manning a road block, flagged down a Renault Dauphine car; inside were four men. Three proffered their identification papers. One, who had no papers at all, was taken to the local police station where he was identified from the files of missing and wanted persons as Pierre Magade, a deserter from the French Air Force. His arrest took place very close to an Air Force base and there was no difficulty in checking his identity; but in view of the night's event in the Paris suburbs, it was decided to take him to the Criminal Brigade headquarters in Lyon to be interrogated. Question after question, all apparently innocent, and concerning his life as a deserter, were put to him. Then came a silence. Then a detective asked suddenly: 'But what about Petit-Clamart?' Magade, a *pied noir,* born, bred and trained in Algeria, confessed.

Within 48 hours most of those who took part in the attempted assassination were arrested, including Bastien-Thiry, then regarded as the leader. Not in custody though, were the equally if not more important participants, Colonel Antoine Argoud and the marksman '*le boiteaux*' or 'the limp', Georges Watin, so-called because of his lameness.

Despite the opposition of the armed forces, and it was estimated that 80% of the graduates of the *École de Guerre* were in fact against de Gaulle and his Algerian policy, the French Government decided that the rebellion should be treated as treason; that a special military court should be set up and that barristers be given back their wartime military ranks to justify their participation. Eventually 52 were appointed as judges, magistrates and legal advisers to man the State Security Court to try the 1,000 people awaiting trial, accused of plotting against the State and/or the life of the

President of the French Republic.

The Court, sitting at the Fort at Vincennes, eventually gave its verdict, rejecting the defence plea that the accused had wanted to take de Gaulle prisoner and try him for illegal acts. Nine men had appeared before the court and the remaining six were sentenced in their absence. The result was that six were sentenced to death and nine sent to prison for terms ranging from three years to life. Of the six sentenced to death three were absent, including the missing Georges Watin. Of the three actually before the court, two (Lieutenant Alain de la Tocnaye, second-in-command, and Jacques Prevost) had their sentences commuted to life imprisonment by the President. He refused to intervene in the case of Bastien-Thiry.

This 36-year-old Lieutenant-Colonel in the French Air Force, who was tried as he wore his blue uniform decorated with the Knight's Cross of the Legion of Honour handed to him personally by the President less than two years previously, faced death. Married, father of three children, he was undoubtedly the most important person in custody. The sentence of death was only a week old when he was awakened in his cell at 4 am and told that his defence lawyers had arrived. He asked, 'Am I the only one to be executed?' The lawyers answered 'Yes.' 'Are the others pardoned?' Again came the answer, 'Yes.'

The Colonel crossed himself, asked for paper and pen, and permission to attend Mass and take Communion. On the paper he sought a reprieve on the grounds that ex-Premier Georges Bidault was held in custody in Germany and could throw authoritative light on the work of OAS and the alleged assassination. When he was told that this argument would not be forwarded he went to the chapel of the Fresnes prison. Afterwards there was coffee, and he was driven to the forbidding Fort d'Ivry. 'I have been condemned illegally and I protest my innocence before my children and my compatriots,' he said. With those words he picked up his rosary and marched on to the parade square of the Fort.

De Gaulle survived every attempt on his life and died peacefully in bed after seeing his policy of an independent Algeria vindicated. Some of his OAS enemies still live on.

There was a quaint, essentially French touch to the execution. The firing-squad had formed up; Bastien-Thiry's last words were, ironically, 'My execution would be an assassination,' before the squad marched past the accused. 'Eyes right' came the command and the man about to die stood stiffly to attention as those about to kill him saluted. He thanked the officer for the offer of a blindfold by shaking his head and saluting, and there rang out a salvo followed by the single shot which killed him.

The Conspiracy Smashed

Other members of the assassination squad were gradually rounded up, the most audacious arrest being that of Colonel Argoud. He had been with other OAS leaders in Algeria, Spain, Rome and Vienna. There was to be a further meeting in Munich and for that purpose Argoud booked a room in the Eden-Wolff hotel. When he arrived at the hotel, there were waiting for him a number of '*les barbouzes*' (the bearded ones), members of the *Service de Documentation Extérieure et de Contre-Espionage* (SDECE) and they were from the élite action squad of that organization. While one asked

if he was in fact Colonel Argoud, and another asked for his papers, a third seized the unsuspecting Colonel in a masterly grip and propelled him through a side-door of the hotel to a waiting car. Although he fought the driver, he was rendered unconscious and woke up 500 miles away in the Criminal Brigade offices in the Quai des Ofevres, Paris.

Paris would naturally receive from Munich protests about this interference with the liberty of a Frenchman on German soil, but the *Service* regarded itself as immune from diplomatic niceties. Having captured Argoud they had him bound and gagged and dumped into a van which was then parked and abandoned in the precincts of the Nôtre Dame Cathedral. Without further ado one of the captors telephoned the police to inform them where the Colonel they were seeking could be found. 'Argoud has betrayed us. He has failed in every mission, especially in assassinating de Gaulle. You can have him,' said 'the bearded one' with wry humour but unchallengeable efficiency.

There were further attempts on de Gaulle's life. In 1963 a sniper armed with a rifle and telescopic sight was to shoot him in the back as he visited the *Ecole Militaire* in Paris. A woman teacher of English, who smoked cigars, was interviewed—in that dramatic way the French have—and, with the help of her address book, revealed the names of the conspirators. Again, Georges Watin was said to be among them. He was not found but, with less than twelve hours to spare, the General's life was again saved. It has been said of him, by M. Soustelle among others, that 'he seldom forgives, he never forgets'. The General, however, reprieved from a death-sentence more people than have been executed, and he knew the truth of the words of M. Francois Mauriac, one of his supporters: 'The fact is that the death penalty has been abolished in the minds and hearts of modern Frenchmen.' The General wanted Bastien-Thiry executed as an example to other rebels, a lesson not to be perpetuated, though. One such execution he hoped would suffice, but the attempts since invited even more penalties.

The General is dead now and immortalized forever in the history of France; but some of the OAS still nurture their dream of a French dominated Algeria. It is they, not de Gaulle, who never forgave and never forgot.

RASPUTIN~ THE POWER BEHIND THE THRONE

In terms of vulnerability, only a Russian could match Charles de Gaulle, such has been the frequency of murder in high places on that great land mass since earliest times. The earliest recorded assassination was before Genghis Khan, the next perhaps tomorrow, the last probably never.

Assassination stalked the earliest princes. Did not a Mongol kill the last of the original assassins by assassination? The Tzars used it and suffered by it. And the Communists of the 20th-century Union of Socialist Soviet Republics have found it necessary, not only for their enemies, but for their comrades, too. It has occurred so frequently that an encyclopedic work would have to be set aside for assassination *à la Russe* alone, if it would be complete.

Yet one of the most famous slayings in Russia is rarely thought of as an assassination. The victim was not a high-born man; he did not hold high office; and he was not an overtly political figure.

A powerful figure, with staring, hypnotic eyes, Gregory Efimovitch Rasputin rose to become the most powerful man in Tzarist Russia.

But he was possibly the most powerful man of his time: his name was Rasputin.

The "Mad Monk"

Gregory Efimovitch Rasputin was born in a village in the Tobolsk province of Siberia in 1871, and lived there for more than 30 years, marrying a local girl who bore him three daughters. He followed no trade, received no formal education, but impressed those around him by a number of characteristics —his hypnotic green eyes, his attraction to women who found him irresistible, and his apparently extravagant piety. These attributes, conflicting though they may appear, guided his future fantastic conduct.

Russia, at the turn of the century, was as much imbued with superstition as with orthodox Christian religion, and the countryside was populated with the *staretz*—the wandering holy men— forever making pilgrimages, healing the sick through prayer and abstinence without being ordained in holy orders or qualified in medical practice. They were as prevalent as *fakirs* in India, hot-gospellers in America, and fortune-tellers in England. There is no direct accurate translation of *staretz*, although they behaved like monks while not necessarily belonging to any order, nor being as holy as those of a monastic calling.

Rasputin visited many monasteries where he received food and shelter, and it was on such an occasion, at the monastery of St Michael, in Kiev, that a chance meeting altered his life. Chopping wood in the courtyard, he was approached by two pilgrims who asked him about his work. Rasputin, bearded and with long hair, stared at them with his mesmeric eyes and told how he could cure the sick by prayer. The pilgrims, the Grand Duchesses Anastasia and Milatza, asked him if he could cure a child suffering from haemophilia. To this, Rasputin is supposed to have described the symptoms of the disease with medical accuracy. Although he might not have known the exact identity of his prospective patient, he could have hazarded a guess that the Grand Duchesses were not inquiring about a cure for the offspring of a peasant.

They were anxious about the health of the Tzarevitch Alexis, fifth child of the Tzar Nicholas and the Tzarina. That is why Rasputin went to St Petersburg.

His arrival was as sensational as his departure. From a Siberian village, this uncouth and dirty wanderer, with the uncombed hair and black fingernails, entered the fabulously wealthy Court of the Romanoffs. With him he took herbs, one of which he claimed he had obtained from a Tibetan magician (named Badmyev), and which could be used to cure haemophilia, but which could also cause mental paralysis.

Thus this agent of good and evil was taken to the bedside of the boy Alexis. Placing his hand on the boy's forehead, he prayed. The boy, who had been melancholy, smiled at the weird stranger, and gradually recovered. With the child's health improving day by day, Rasputin was accepted. He could visit the palace every day and, with the child's mother devoted to him, his ambitions could be fulfilled. He would advise the Tzarina, who would then tell her weak-minded husband, Nicholas, what to do; and the monk would, in that way, become the virtual ruler of Russia.

A Depraved Influence

That dictatorship from behind the throne was to take place despite the depravity of the new influence, who was a lecher, a drunk and the inventor of orgies determined to outdo even the debauchery of the Russian Court into which he had been admitted. He had learnt about lechery while travelling with a strange sect of *staretz* known as *Khlystys*. These spiritualistic believers held lovefeasts, in which there were absolutely free relations between all brothers and sisters. They had their 'virgins' appointed to receive the adoration of followers, and permitted flagellation in some of their ceremonies. Not surprisingly, they had numerous followers, particularly in central Russia.

They believed that a man must sin in order to be purified by prayer; and the greater the sinfulness, the greater and more absolute would be the absolution from his sins. This teaching Rasputin took to the Tzarkoie Selo, the imperial Buckingham Palace in the St Petersburg suburbs. To the converts and devotees, almost entirely women, he would explain that his religion demanded total private obedience. With his hypnotic eyes, he would lure them to his private quarters, where their initiation into the mysteries of saintliness through sin would begin. Invariably they had to unclothe Rasputin, put him into a bath, and wash him as a preliminary cleansing ceremony. They were then seduced, encouraged to get drunk, to behave in an abandoned fashion, to glorify in any depravity, and then, when sober, confess their sins to Rasputin. After that they could begin to sin again.

He conducted these orgies with monotonous regularity; was accused of raping a nun; was seen walking openly in the nude with a nude woman outside a brothel; and although he brought his wife and family to live in St Petersburg, he kept eleven women in the same house at the same time.

Any criticism of Rasputin brought the wrath of the royal household on the critic. His word was law, and many who crossed him were sent to Siberia as punishment. Newspapers were forbidden to publicly criticize him, on pain of being put out of business by the censor. Courtiers and deputies from the Duma, anxious for royal favour or ministerial posts, could hope for nothing if they challenged the influence of the depraved peasant turned monk. Even the Tzar's orders were likely to be baulked when Rasputin advised contrary decisions to the Tzarina, the life of whose son he had saved.

Rasputin's Power Grows

In the royal household at this time was a comparative newcomer, Prince Felix Youssoupoff. An Oxford graduate, the son of an aide-de-camp to the Tzar, he married in February 1914, at the age of

27, the Tzar's niece, Her Highness Irene Alexandrovna, Princess of Russia and daughter of the Grand Duke Alexander Michaelovitch. The Prince was never a strong person physically, but was fanatically devoted to his wife. He belonged to one of the oldest and noblest Russian households, the Sumarakoff–Elsten family. One of their womenfolk had been abducted by Ivan the Terrible, and one of their earliest remembered members had fought for his land against the Golden Horde.

When the newlyweds arrived together at the

Rasputin with fishermen in Siberia. This remote region was the home of a sect of religious fanatics who taught Rasputin the art of faith-healing and the power of hypnosis.

court for the first time, Rasputin was suffering banishment for his misdemeanours. An English governess retained to watch over the four royal princesses had complained about his behaviour and had demanded that Rasputin be kept out of the young girls' bedrooms. This and similar outrageous conduct had forced the Tzar and Tzarina to exile him, albeit temporarily. His letters to the Tzarina pleaded to be allowed to return. The Tzarina, in her replies, used all the words she knew to express her reproaches for his conduct, her vehement belief in his godliness, and her personal affection. He could return.

Against his influence over the Tzarina the Tzar had no weapon. When the Tzar spoke to a minister, he gave the commands of the Tzarina who passed on the orders from Rasputin. Thus, no one could brook the decrees from 'Anny's little house'—the name given to Anna Vryubova's villa of softly furnished rooms near the royal palace. There among the cushions the affairs of State were settled, and there Rasputin elevated the grand-daughter of Queen Victoria from being a rather shy, domestic woman, to an imperious madonna worthy of the rank of Tzarina in her own right. He had saved her son's life. He had given her the confidence of a queen. No wonder that she could not bring herself to believe the accusations against him, nor acknowledge the baleful influence some people said that he exercised over Russian society. Rasputin was her friend. If he was wrong, she did not want to know about it, and was ecstatic when he was proved correct.

High-born aristocratic women of St Petersburg society, queued with beggars and the diseased to see him, feel his touch and receive his blessings. If they believed that he was responsible for the fall of the Grand Duke Nicholas, former commander-in-chief of the Russian armies; if he was the instigator of the plot to assassinate M. Miliuhoff, leader of the Cadet party in the Duma; and if he was for or against the dismissal of the Prime Minister Sturmer, he must have had good reason and worthy motives. Not that they could possibly have believed all his prophecies, which included the wartime upheaval of the political regime and the denouement of the revolution. It was sufficient

Below left *Such was Rasputin's influence with the Royal Family, that the most powerful figures in the land courted his favour.*

Below *Prince Felix Youssoupoff with his wife, Irene. The Prince feared that she might succumb to the sexually powerful Rasputin.*

Right *The Russian Royal Family. Months after Rasputin's death they were brutally murdered.*

that Rasputin, the Richelieu of Russia, should be behind the throne to speak and act.

First Death Bid

Fortunately, perhaps, Rasputin was away from the orbit of the throne when he was most needed, at the time of the outbreak of World War One. He had taken his son Dmitry back to his home village of Pokrovsky in Siberia. While walking by the post-office, a beggar asked for alms (according to the official story), and when Rasputin went to give the supplicant alms a woman attacked him. The woman, Guseva, from Tzaritsin, produced a knife with a 21-inch blade and stabbed the lay monk. She was seized, and only a strong escort prevented her from being lynched. She was taken to prison, where she attempted suicide, and where she gave several reasons for her attempt to assassinate the famous figure. She alternately wanted to revenge local Siberian girls he had corrupted; to rid Russia of Rasputin in favour of her own favourite monk, one Iliodor; to prevent Rasputin preaching the gospels of 'an anti-Christ'; simply to remove his bad influence on the Tzar and Tzarina. Whatever the reasons, she had followed him to Yalta, to St Petersburg, and to his Siberian birthplace, where he had deliberately avoided her until this dramatic moment.

Rasputin recovered in the hospital at neighbouring Tiumen, but his curious request to see his would-be assassin at his bedside was refused by the authorities.

The Tzarina, proud, unbending, confident of her God-given right to rule, with her husband, the Tzar, a cardboard model of a guards officer at her side, publicly denounced the attempt on Rasputin's life. When asked about the monk's influence, the Emperor Nicholas II would only say that it would be better to have five Rasputins than one hysterical woman. They needed Rasputin. And when they needed him most, after the Sarajevo incident which preceded World War I, he was still in hospital. There is ample evidence that if he had been at Court at that time, his own pro-German sympathies, plus those of the Tzarina, would have inspired him to prevent the Tzar from signing the mobilization order.

During the first year of the war, there was a very great deal of pro-German activity in political circles in St Petersburg, and Rasputin's influence and the success of that activity leave no doubt that he was pro-German. This has been taken to be the only reason for the next attack on his life. That is not so. Prince Youssoupoff, during the Christmas celebrations of 1916, heard a considerable number of stories about the monk's orgiastic rituals and his method of corrupting young women. 'You think I am defiling you, but I am not,' he would tell them. 'I am purifying you.' The young Prince, highly impressionable, and highly nervous at the prospect of his young wife falling for such a mountebank, sought advice on what he should do.

The Party

The outcome was that Rasputin was invited to a wild party in the cellar of the Prince's home on the Moika Canal on December 29. His influence had not waned, but his public following had suffered under the weight of rumours about his pro-German sympathies. Even the police had warned him to be

on guard against assassins, whether motivated by personal animosity or by revolutionary zeal. The Prince was expecting him; but should he go? His own daughter, Maria, tried to persuade him not to go. She and another daughter, Vavara, hid his boots on that night to prevent him going out and risking his life. After all he was hated on several counts, not the least of which was his secret attempts to negotiate a separate peace treaty with the Germans and without the other allies, news of which had reached the gossips and was later to be confirmed by officials.

The Prince's wife, Irene, was beautiful and she had never met Rasputin although he must have heard about her, and it is, on balance, probable that he was either invited because she was supposed to be definitely attending the party, or that he accepted believing that she would be present. There is no question that the Princess took any part in the organization of the party, the invitations, the arrangements, or the guests. She had been suffering from influenza and was, at the time, con-

Rasputin holds 'court'. The aristocratic women of St Petersburg flocked to the 'mad monk'. He preached a 'religion' which offered salvation through sin – his 'services' turned into orgies.

valescing in the Crimea. The Prince always denied that he used his wife in any way as a bait. Even so, he was known to fear Rasputin and dread what effect the 'mad monk', as he was known, would have on such a beautiful bride of less than three years. If they ever met, what then?

The Prince had already made up his mind. He had consulted the Grand Duke Dmitri Pavlovitch, the Tzar's favourite cousin; Dr Lazovert, a military doctor; Lieutenant Shoukotine; and a right-wing member of the Duma, Deputy Pourich-kevich. The doctor had provided cyanide, which had been mixed in six small cakes, three almond and three chocolate which were the monk's favourites, and which had been used to 'spike' the Madeira wine to which he was also devoted. Such planning was not foolproof against the principal guest's suspicions. He hesitated before eating the cakes and asked for fresh plates because those on the table appeared to have been used; they had been rinsed in cyanide.

A phonograph was playing the old hit-tune, *Yankee Doodle Dandy*, and Rasputin, presumably to liven the party, asked the Prince to give an accompaniment on a guitar, which he did, watching the lay monk all the time. He watched his guest with amazement as Rasputin ate the cakes, all six of them, and then, filling and refilling his glass, emptied a complete bottle with no apparent ill effects. If he showed any symptoms they were those of the influence of alcohol and not, surprisingly, of cyanogen and its compounded poison.

Above *A rather fanciful view of Rasputin's death. The monk, to the horror of his assassins, survived the attempt to poison him with cyanide.*

Inset *Rasputin in death. Despite attempts to cover up the crime, the recovery of his body from the River Neva led to a massive scandal.*

A Macabre Scene

This fantastic scene should be halted at that moment, as Rasputin got up to dance, to explain the reason for this state of affairs. Potassium cyanide, as was used in this case, in the quantities described, should have killed and killed quickly. Rasputin, though, suffered from alcoholic gastritis, a kind of dyspepsia in which the stomach fails to secrete acid. The stomach normally, in 95 cases out of every 100, secretes hydrochloric acid, and that acid must be there before the cyanide compound can act. Without that acid Rasputin could not be poisoned.

At this, the Prince, without medical knowledge, unable to understand the failure of the deadly poison, drew the monk's attention to a very beautiful ivory crucifix which stood on the cabinet at the far end of the room. When the chosen guest was examining it, Prince Felix produced a revolver and shot the royal adviser in the side. Rasputin fell, but as the Prince knelt beside him, the eylids opened and the attacker found the hypnotic eyes, with their peculiar but powerful attraction, staring at him. Before the Prince could move, the victim, in his long kaftan of blue serge, grabbed his assailant by the throat. The struggle completely unnerved the handsome young Prince, who managed to free himself from the weakened monk and ran from the room, only to find himself pursued by the fantastically agile Rasputin on all fours.

At that moment, the Prince's fellow conspirators rushed down from the upstairs room. As Rasputin reached the courtyard, the Grand Duke produced his service revolver and shot the hated Svengali in the chest, while another fired a shot into Rasputin's head. The Prince, to make doubly sure, picked up an iron bar and beat his victim mercilessly until the body was completely still. Yet, even then, as the Prince gazed down on the lifeless body, one non-seeing hypnotic eye stared back at him, and the Prince collapsed into the arms of his servants.

It was 3 am, and at that moment two policemen, one patrolling the Moika Canal, the other in Offitserskya Street, rushed to the front entrance of the princely residence in Corokhovaya Street. There they were handed 1,000 roubles bribe and, when they were asked about the incident by their superiors, they dutifully reported that their Excellencies were in high spirits and had just dispatched a dog. If they had waited, they would have seen a motor-car arrive and the body of Rasputin, wrapped in a fur coat, pushed inside and driven away. Then, at the mouth of a tributary of the River Neva, near Petrovsky island, the peasant from Siberia, who rose to become the *eminence grise* of Russia, left this life through a hole in the ice. The man who called the Emperor 'Papa' and the Empress 'Mama', and used the familiar address, 'thou', which was forbidden even Grand Dukes, was no more.

Aftermath

But the assassination could not be silenced. Rasputin's daughters had reported his disappearance, his bloodstained clothing had been seen by servants, as had the body, and the tell-tale blood trail and galoshes found on the bank of the River Neva, told more of the story. Soon his body appeared in the water. His bonds had been broken and his arms were outstretched like the crossbars of the Cross. He was secretly re-buried, and even when his body was exhumed by a suspicious army officer from beneath a wooden chapel near the imperial residence, no further action was taken.

Saved from trial but fearing the revolution, Prince Youssoupoff and his wife escaped from the Crimea in a British warship in the following year, and settled in London, Paris and New York. He sold in America the Rembrandts he had brought with him from Russia, opened a perfumery salon in Mayfair, London, and practised faith-healing in Paris. He engaged in a number of lawsuits over his life-story, won some and lost some, and was planning a repeat performance of the assassination for television when, in 1967, he died in New York at the age of 81.

The assassination contributed nothing to the 1917 revolution, although Rasputin is credited with prophesying the end of the old order. While he healed the haemophilic son of the Tzar, he once declared that if anything happened to him the boy would die. He foretold that, if he died, his death would be followed by that of the royal family. Eighteen months after his death, the Tzar, Tzarina and their family were shot at Ekaterinburg.

TROTSKY~
VICTIM OF STALIN

Lev Davidovitch Bronstein became Leon Trotsky and, with Vladimir Ilyich Lenin, founded the Soviet Union. After Lenin died in 1924, the struggle for the leadership of the Communist State was between Trotsky and Josef Stalin; Stalin won. Trotsky had to flee Russia to escape Stalin's intention to liquidate him. He went to sanctuary after sanctuary, only to find Soviet agents not far behind him, until he reached Norway. There he was pursued by diplomatic agents, until Norway had to expel him to his final asylum in Mexico.

It was January 1937, and by this time Mexico's protesters, the *descalzados* and *descamisados* (the shoeless and the shirtless), had been replaced by another type of dissenter—the increasingly highly organized members of the Communist Party of Mexico. The party paid lip service to the revolutionary left-wing Government of President Cardenas, pretended that their differences were really very narrow, and looked forward to the day when it could infiltrate and take over the Government. Cardenas, however, was not deceived by this kind of propaganda, and part of his answer to the Communists was to grant Trotsky asylum in Mexico.

By this time, a series of purges in Russia had discredited and vilified Trotsky, and he had been sentenced to death *in absentia*. The world has often been told that Stalin personally ordered and, by remote control, supervised the execution by assassination. But there are many unanswered questions. Why did it take more than three years before a Spaniard tricked his way into Trotsky's heavily fortified sanctuary—a villa on the Avenida Viena, in the Coyoacan suburb of Mexico City—and, wielding an ice axe, killed Trotsky? And, even knowing that the assassin was an avowed Com-

Leon Trotsky – a portrait of the man in power. His influence on left wing revolutionary groups posed a direct threat to Stalin.

munist, can it be true that he was schooled, trained and especially sent to Mexico by the *Narodnyi Komissariat Vniutrenikh Del* (NKVD), the People's Commissariat of Internal Affairs, in order to carry out a piece of butchery that would have been more appropriate in an abattoir? If he was so prepared for the task, which would have had to take months of preparation and planning, why were there no adequate arrangements for his own escape after the killing?

Long Arm of Stalin

Trotsky had to be killed—Marshall Stalin had so decreed. He claimed that Trotsky was bent on destroying the Union of Soviet Socialist Republics (USSR), from the Presidium to the people themselves; but the truth was that he feared Trotsky's pen. Stalin invented the myth that Trotsky was powerful, with offices in every major city in the world, with paid espionage agents, and that his sole object was the destruction of Russia. The truth was that Trotsky's persuasive pen was the menace. Bernard Shaw said of him: 'When he cuts off his opponent's head, he holds it up to show that there are no brains in it.'

Only two organizations, in Communist eyes, could stop that pen—the NKVD through its foreign section *Glavnoye Upravlenye Gosudarstvennoy Besopasnosti* (GUGB), the Chief Directorate of State Security, and the Mexican Communist Party. The NKVD had been very active at the time of the Spanish Civil War; they collected as many passports of the living and the dead as they could. One of these was destined for the future assassin of Trotsky.

The passport belonged to a naturalized Canadian from Yugoslavia who, as Tony Banich, went to Spain, enrolled in the International Brigade of left-wing sympathizers, and was killed in 1936 in the early days of that bloody brother-against-brother conflict. His passport found its way into the possession of Ramon Mercader, a Catalan from Barcelona, but with a new, strange name—Frank Jacson.

The Mexican Communist Party had no such advantage of power, size or organization. Few of its members could be entrusted with such a deed as assassination, although Diego Rivera, the famous painter, was mentioned. He had (during a temporary dispute with the Party) boasted that he had in fact lured Trotsky so that he could be assassinated.

The NKVD, on the other hand, had a very real reputation in the field of liquidation. During the 1920s, 1930s and afterwards, enemies of the Soviet Union disappeared, were kidnapped, were found shot dead, or appeared to have committed suicide without the police in the countries to which they had fled ever tracing those responsible. NKVD men who quit the service of Stalin while on overseas missions were experts in arranging disguises and disappearances, yet figured most prominently on the list of those liquidated. Ignace Reiss, one such official, was found shot dead in Lausanne. Another, General Walter Krivitsky, was found shot dead in a Washington DC hotel room in circumstances which were meant to suggest suicide, but which were undoubtedly created by an assassin.

Even Trotsky's own secretary, Erwin Wolf, had been murdered when he went from Norway to Spain ahead of his master's exile. Only a year after Trotsky's arrival in Mexico, the artist Diego had to break the news to him that his 32-year-old son, Leon Sedov had died in Paris. Leon had been taken to hospital with abdominal pains, protected by friends, registered in the name of Martin, posing as an engineer instead of a political refugee, and admitted for an appendectomy. The operation was successful but, inexplicably, he was found wandering in his pyjamas in a delirium from which he never recovered. He died—another victim of the NKVD.

An Unlikely Assassin

With such a successful record of remote-control murder, it is more than difficult to accept without question that Moscow chose Ramon Mercader,

alias Frank Jacson, especially for the task of killing Leon Trotsky. He was five feet ten-inches tall, and wiry; he wore spectacles to correct both short-sightedness and astigmatic defects, and was partly deaf. While otherwise physically fit for his 26 years, he was temperamentally and psychologically a risk for any espionage or counter-espionage organization to employ. He was born on February 7, 1914, and his background suggests instability. His mother, who had a strong influence on him, was separated from his father and took the family— four brothers and a sister—first to Toulouse, then Bordeaux, before returning to Barcelona. Ramon had been sent to a school for hotel boys at Lyons, became an assistant chef at the Ritz, Barcelona, and was known for little more than that he carved well. His mother, meanwhile, had been popping in and out of bed with a prominent French Communist, had become converted, and was carrying out tasks for the French Communist Party, which she would later teach her son, Ramon. Both his next occupation and the political climate of Spain were ideal for him to receive such instruction. Alfonso XIII had fled, was superseded by the republican-socialist coalition, and anarchist-syndicalist factions in Barcelona were ready for rebellion. Ramon did not wait to be called up for National Service, but volunteered, and in the Jaen Infantry Regiment he rose rapidly from private to sergeant. By the time he left the Army, two years later in 1934, he was ready to join the rebels in street-fighting— although organizational work under the guise of the Cervantes Artistic Recreational Circle, and similar 'front' organizations on behalf of the Communists, was more to his liking. By the time the Spanish Civil War began he had already spent short periods in prison in Barcelona and Valencia for alleged breaches of public order, but without being given a specific sentence. The Popular Front took over from the ineffectual government; Ramon was released, and General Franco, commanding troops in Spanish Morocco, announced that he would march against the new government.

Although Ramon's mother, Caridad, was an avowed Communist, organized the Communist

Left Ramon Mercador, alias Jacques Mornard, alias Frank Jacson, with his Communist agent mother, Caridad.

Women's Union from a waterfront hotel, and took her sons as the first volunteers for the Popular Front Republican forces to fight Franco, their actual Communist involvement from that moment seems vague. Caridad was wounded and was sent to Mexico on a mission. She is said to have been sent by the Republicans to gain support for their cause in Mexico, although she travelled with others on forged passports. She is said, alternatively, to have been sent, on direct orders from Moscow, to find out everything about Trotsky. This is impossible since her mission to, and return from, Mexico were accomplished in 1936. Trotsky did not arrive in that country until January 9 of the following year.

On her return to Europe she no doubt continued her Communist schooling of Ramon, an invalided lieutenant from the republican forces, but to what extent that schooling was carried out can only be a case for speculation. He is supposed to have attended a Barcelona school of terrorism, which had some 600 pupils. He is supposed to have been sent to Moscow for training and there hand-picked for the assassination of Trotsky. He is supposed to have undergone training in murder, blowing up railroads, intelligence, sabotage and guerilla warfare. And he is supposed to have been a first-class pupil and favourite for the assassination to come.

It is curious, therefore, that he should have undertaken such menial tasks, and extremely roundabout jobs, before Trotsky's death. He went to Paris, and there by design, or chance, he met Sylvia Ageloff, one of three sisters whose home was in New York. She was there to attend an allegedly secret meeting of world delegates to the Fourth International. Mercader, alias Jacson, now alias Jacques Mornard, was hovering around at the time. He was introduced to Sylvia, a Trotsky courier, and with his dashing grandee manners he had little difficulty in proposing to her.

An Implausible Agent

Ramon told his fiancée many implausible stories: that he was a writer; that he could sell her stories to a secret agency; that he had to be absent to attend to family victims of a car accident in Brussels;

that he had fled to England to escape military draft in Belgium; that his father had been an important diplomat; and that one of his absences was due to being imprisoned for desertion from the army. If he was a writer, she never saw his work. If he sold her stories secretly it was so that she did not sell direct to publishers and cut out the agent's commission. When he explained that his father had been killed in the road accident, he had to write to her later to say that this was not true and that only the chauffeur had been killed. His father was not in the car, having got out to go to the toilet, when a ten ton lorry hit the car, killing the chauffeur and seriously injuring his mother. Again he was believed. The trusting fiancée did not check on the status or whereabouts of the alleged father-diplomat, nor on the father's reaction when he heard that his son was an unpatriotic deserter. This then was the accomplished person who sought to enter the Americas. He told her that the Belgians would let him go abroad without serving military service, but also that he, a diplomat's son, was having difficulty in obtaining an American visa. Then, equally suddenly and equally implausible he arrived in New York. World War Two was only ten days away.

Stalin believed that it was a capitalist war in which the great capitalist powers would exhaust each other. He believed that workers' revolutions would then take place throughout Europe: the Soviet Union had only to sit back and wait. His NKVD suddenly became so active, under the new command of the feared and hated Lavrenti Beria, that they sent many of their people, including Ramon's mother, to the Americas; either first to the USA, or direct to Mexico, to carry out the long-awaited operation of eliminating Leon Trotsky.

Not only were Mercader's stories unbelievable, but his behaviour was almost certain to draw attention to himself. Ostentatiously, he struck up a friendship with an official of an airways corporation and boasted of his mountain-climbing abilities. Since arriving in Mexico he had scaled, on his own, the 18,700 feet Citlaltepetl, and when could he have an opportunity to tackle Popocatepetl (17,881

Right *Trotsky in exile was more dangerous than Trotsky in the USSR; while he lived, Stalin could never feel secure.*

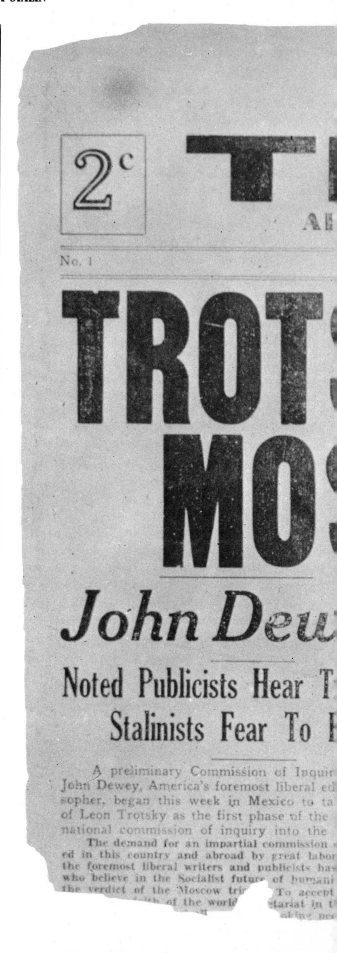

RUTH
THE MOSCOW TRIALS

Published by
PIONEER PUBLISHERS
100 Fifth Ave., New York
Bundle orders 1c per 100
Send checks or money
order with order

Editor MAX SHACHTMAN

NEW YORK, N. Y.   APRIL, 1937

KY BARES
COW FRAUD

Heads Mexico Inquiry

HE DOES NOT CONFESS!

ONLY TRUTH CAN UNMASK FRAME-UP

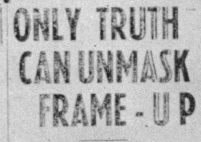

ssue

by Dr.
philo
stimony
interials.
supportions and
at those
accept
let is to
Revolu

"These pages seek to tell the truth about the Moscow trials, the most infamous frame-ups in history.

S. M. Kirov, head of the Leningrad Communist Party was assassinated on Dec. 1, 1934. In the ensuing weeks 120 men de-feet)? When he did join a group on such an expedition, he pleaded fatigue and an ankle injury, and left the lesser mountaineers to go ahead.

Where the suggestion that Ramon Mercader was the chosen assassin really fails belongs to the night of May 23 and 24. By this time, the carefully prepared Ramon had only got as far as the gates of the fortified Trotsky villa, to deliver goods for a sick friend, to collect the sick friend and take him to hospital and return him to the villa, in order to try to get chatting to the guards. But on this night, even with the allegedly senior NKVD men in Mexico, the Mexican Communists themselves decided to assassinate Trotsky.

Trotsky's Villa Stormed

Again fact and fiction must merge, because the Comintern had only recently ordered a change of power at the top of the satellite Mexican Communist Party. Leaders were removed from office and the pro-Russian hard-line party members were put in charge. So, while the ruthless NKVD machine was actually in Mexico, it allowed the Mexicans, under new leadership, to carry out the attempted assassination. What happened was farcical. Two Communist girl spies lured the Mexican police—ordered to guard Trotsky by the President himself—to a party. The girls then passed on information about the villa to the painter, David Alfaro Siqueiros, and his reconnoitring associates. Eventually some 20 men in four motor cars, carrying sub-machine guns, incendiary bombs, explosive bombs, rope ladders, gaffs and hooks, even a rotary power saw, and official police uniforms, began to move towards the fortified villa.

The police were away. There was no guard at the machine gun tower at the corner of the villa facing the converging streets. When an American guard, the wealthy Sheldon Harte, a 23-year-old devotee of Trotsky, opened the gate, the 24 attackers rushed in, firing sub-machine guns, their Mauser pistols, flinging home-made firebombs at the windows and hoping their three pound dynamite bomb would wreck the house. When 73 bullets had been pumped into Trotsky's own bedroom and the explosive bomb smashed the door between that bedroom and the adjoining room of

Above *David Alfaro Siqueiros, a painter of renown, executed the first assassination attempt.*

his grandson, the attackers decided to pull out, satisfied that their work was done. They had cut the telephone wires and the electric alarm between the villa and the police headquarters. What more could they expect?

They took Harte away with them and he was found dead in a ditch some time later, but Mr and Mrs Trotsky and their grandson were unharmed. When the firing began they heard their grandson, Seva, cry out and they crept into his room pulling him out of his bed. They then lay close together in a corner of the room out of range of the crossfire which raked the ceilings. Mrs Trotsky got up to beat out the flames caused by the incendiaries, burning her hands in the attempt.

There is little doubt that the assassination attempt compromised both the Soviet and Mexican Communist camps. The Russians blamed the Mexican Communist leaders, and the Mexican Communist leaders blamed those whom they had recently ousted from office. They even denounced Siqueiros as an uncontrollable half-mad element in fringe circles. He and his associates had conveniently left the country. But what was to be discovered next could not be brushed aside. Siqueiros and his aides had taken a house to which the young American, Harte, had been taken and there had been shot, probably while asleep, and his body dumped in a lime-filled grave. When the grave gave up the remains and the stench of putrefying flesh, Trotsky was called to identify the body of his bodyguard. When that news was published the stupefaction turned to horror. There had been a suggestion that the assassination attempt was a phoney 'inside job' which Trotsky had staged to draw public attention to his cause and to publicise the book about Stalin which he was writing. There had also been some disbelief that the attempt at assassination, if carried out by others, had been a serious sortie against Trotsky's life, or merely an anti-Trotsky propaganda move, to boost the Communists' strength, and perhaps steal his anti-Stalin manuscripts and other archives. The murder of Sheldon Harte proved to the public that all this was wrong: there had been an attempt on Trotsky's life and the assassins meant business.

Colonel Leandro A. Sanchez Salazar, chief of the Mexican Secret Police, had decided that this was not a genuine assassination attempt and had arrested some of Trotsky's own guards to prove it, until Trotsky intervened with President Cardenas who ordered their release. He then went to work on the contrary information and soon arrested a large number of hirelings who had been involved in the attack on the villa and the killing of Harte. After that the Colonel, the President and the public

Below *The exiled Trotsky in relaxed mood.*

generally did not believe that there would be another attempt on the exile's life. Trotsky must have been resigned to it. He personally supervised the fantastic security precautions of the villa when it was rebuilt after the gun and bomb attack, and made sure that anyone who opened the bedroom door would automatically receive bullets which would be fatal. Yet, when the guards wanted to search his own friends, Trotsky refused.

Brutal Liquidation

He looked for friends he could trust, and he even looked to Ramon Mercader who, by his friendship with Sylvia, the courier, and other Trotskyists within the villa entourage, had been able to gain admittance. Mercader told the Trotskyists as many tall and far-fetched stories as he had to outsiders. Yet Trotsky listened to Ramon when he talked about articles on the Fourth International that he promised to write; and Trotsky declared that Ramon might indeed make an ideal follower, if not a great Trotskyist. But, at the same time Trotsky told one of his aides that, 'one agent of the Stalinists could come here as a friend and assassinate me.'

That was to happen in the late afternoon of August 20, 1940. It was hot, but 'Jacson' wore a hat and a raincoat. He had recently boasted that with an ice-axe he could smash a heavy block of ice with two blows. This day he carried the ice-axe, with its twelve inch handle and seven inch pick-type steel head, in his raincoat pocket, and his mountaineering hammer, with its forked head, attached to his raincoat by a cord. In his trousers he carried a fully loaded .45 Estrella Spanish automatic with an eight-bullet clip in the handle and one bullet hand-fed into the breech.

He had left Sylvia, with whom he had been living in Mexico City, and he drove alone to the villa where by now he was known as 'Sylvia's husband'. People who saw him that day thought he was preoccupied, somewhat bilious looking—although this might have been due to Mexico City's altitude. No one asked why he was going to Trotsky's villa again—the fourth time in barely a fortnight.

He drove his car to Coycoan for the last time, but instead of parking with the bumper to the wall beneath the guard tower, he made a U-turn and pointed the car the way he had come. The electrically operated double doors were opened for him and he was taken to see Trotsky who was at the hutches feeding his rabbits. Trotsky's wife, Natalia, thought it strange that 'Sylvia's husband' should call again so soon without an appointment. The guards thought it strange that the newcomer should ask, 'Has Sylvia arrived yet?' Since Sylvia had no appointment and nor had he. But Trotsky invited 'Jacson' to stay to a meal.

The visitor declined, complaining of not feeling well, and Trotsky, after painstakingly feeding his rabbits, actually invited Ramon into his study to look again at an article Ramon had written. Natalia accompanied them both to the door of the study, where Trotsky sat down within arm's reach of his .38 Colt revolver and a .25 automatic. The alarm switch which could bring the guards was within fingertip reach. But Trotsky began to read the article. Ramon had put his raincoat down on the same desk, removing, as he did so, the short ice-axe, and as he recounted later: 'I took it in my fist and, closing my eyes, I gave him a tremendous blow on the head.'.

As Ramon tried to wield the *poilet* a second time, Trotsky, although 63 years old, grabbed the assassin's hand and bit it to try to make him drop the weapon. His glasses smashed as he fell, but he clutched the door-post and staggered to the drawing-room, thinking he had been shot. In quick time, three guards rushed to the scene. 'Jacson!' cried Trotsky, and the assassin, grasping his automatic now hanging limply in his hand was brought down by one of the guards. Trotsky was not to die yet. 'See what they have done . . . Jacson shot me with a revolver . . . I am seriously wounded . . . I feel that this time it is the end . . . We talked about French statistics . . . Natasha, I love you . . . Seva must be taken away from all this . . . I understood what he wanted to do . . . He wanted to strike me . . . once more and more but I didn't let him . . . I didn't let him, did I? . . .' At this the old man of the Revolution was asked about Jacson being killed. His eyes brightened as he replied, 'Impermissible to kill, he must be . . . forced . . . to . . . talk.' The exile spoke the last three words very slowly and distinctly—already the butts of the guards' guns were working on the head and body of Ramon Mercader, alias Jacson, who was soon unconscious.

Both the assassin and the dying man were taken, ironically, to the same hospital, the Green Cross, where police brought a distraught Sylvia to hear what her husband had done. In that moment she must have wondered whether this was why he had met her in Paris; why he had pursued her to New York; why he had brought her to Mexico: was it so he could be near her when she visited Trotsky in whom she believed, and why he had promised eventually to marry her . . .because he was an agent of the Soviet Union? But was he?

A Tangled Web

In boasting of the death of Trotsky, which occurred 26 hours later, the Russians have let it be known that the glorious mother of the glorious assassin was waiting in a car at the corner of the villa, so that Ramon did not need his car; and that at yet another intersection, Eitingon, alias General Kotov, was waiting for another car switch with his motorcar engine idling all the while. Ramon had been equipped with $890, plus another weapon, a fourteen inch dagger. He had sufficient money to get out of the country but, curiously, he had no passport. Of course, Kotov and/or Caridad, his mother, would have arranged his departure. Caridad left via Guatemala, while the senior NKVD officer is supposed to have driven to Acapulco where a Soviet freighter was conveniently waiting to take him home to Russia.

It is known that Caridad eventually arrived in Moscow where, despite her horror at finding that Kotov, who had been her lover, was married and had a family, she was feted as the mother of a hero and handed, by Stalin personally, the Order of Lenin for her son's courage and bravery in eliminating Trotsky, the dangerous enemy of the people. Stalin also promised that no effort would be spared in rescuing her son from imprisonment in Mexico City.

If we are to ask the motives of Ramon in assassinating Trotsky, we can only do so in a critical manner, since the evidence produced during the last few years has been very largely biased and prejudicial towards one political interest or another. To attract support for the anti-Trotsky

cause when he was alive, the Russians claimed that he was a Nazi or a Fascist, but when Germany invaded the Soviet Union he was a tool of American Imperialism. That he was a Nazi or Fascist, was used to sway Republican forces in Spain who were fighting Nazi and Fascist elements in support of Franco. And, since Ramon was a Republican supporter of the Popular Front, he might well have been influenced by this propaganda.

But there is no evidence to show that he was taken to Moscow, and there schooled and trained for the specific purpose of assassinating Trotsky at his exiled villa 'prison' at Coycoan, Mexico City. He was, in prison in Mexico, to be subjected to some of the most searching psychiatric and psychological tests known to medicine, and these, together with physical observations, handwriting specimens, his answers to many questions put to him, his behaviour before and after the assassination, and many other pieces of evidence, show that no espionage organisation would have ever seriously considered employing him to carry out an international assassination of such tremendous audacity

Above *Detectives hold up the murder weapon – an ice-axe. The clumsy and brutal manner in which Trotsky was murdered led to speculation that Mercador was not an NKVD member.*

Inset *The room in which Trotsky was killed.*

and consequence. If he had failed, and had revealed that the NKVD were behind the assassination, the government action against Communists would have been greater than it was. Since he succeeded, clumsily and brutally, and was arrested, what did it matter to the Soviet Union except that Trotsky was dead and another hero born?

The Real Culprit

Caridad, who originated, not from Spain, as was originally thought, but from Santiago, Cuba, was the real culprit. She came of a well-bred, quite well-to-do family, but from an early age she wanted adventure. By the time of the Spanish Civil War, she had found her aristocratic relatives and in-laws stuffy, and preferred to mix with the new intellectuals who read Marx and other revolutionary writers. It is almost certain that she wanted to ape the well-known La Passionaria, the bomb-tossing communist heroine who came from the Asturias and who was later to be also honoured in Moscow. She proved this when she took her sons to the volunteer office of the Republican forces, but after her own injury, her mission to Mexico and her return, she had to remain in exile. In Paris she lived with a series of Communist leaders, and delighted parties by describing their nude peculiarities. It was there that she probably met Kotov and, in her ambition to become a better communist heroine, decided to throw in her lot with him.

He was an NKVD leader and he was an expert in the liquidation game, and it is certain that he used his influence on Caridad to get certain jobs accomplished, but it is beyond belief that he would choose, accept or approve Caridad's son for such a task as the elimination of Trotsky. What is more likely is that he would accept Caridad's help in getting her son to spy out the land and house of Trotsky for an efficient assassination attempt before or after the bungling amateur effort of Siqueiros. This would enable someone of Kotov's organisation to get the necessary information before carrying out the project. Thus, the Soviet agents would be able to emulate their great activities in the art of assassination during the earlier 1930s. Certainly they would not attempt to kill such a violent enemy of Marshal Stalin with one blow with a shortened ice-axe.

The author does not propose to dwell at any length on the 1,359 pages of the report of Ramon's background, his environmental circumstances, health, activities and abilities which went to the magistrate in the case. It is sufficient to note that in the early stages of his examination, his words, when related to checkable facts, were untrue. Even his age of 36 at the time of his arrest was an exaggeration of some nine or ten years. His alternating stories of why he killed Trotsky did not ring true, since he kept correcting and contradicting himself, just as an unaccomplished liar would. He was alternately a sympathiser of Trotsky, then a dedicated member of the NKVD. First he told how many, many times he had been with Trotsky, until the police produced the visitor's book of the villa. He was not a Russian, he agreed, but nevertheless Trotsky wanted him to assassinate Stalin, but then he had realised that Trotsky was wrong and that he himself should personally assassinate Trotsky. He even repeated his story about being a deserter or draft-dodger of the Belgian Army, and had decided that, rather than face a firing squad back in Brussels, he would obey the orders of his NKVD commanders. Unfortunately, there was no check on his Belgian non-career in the Army, nor could his word be accepted that he was acting

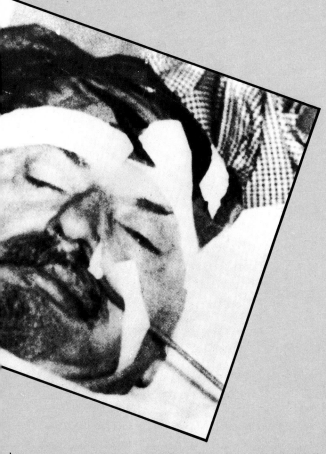

Left *Ramon Mercador seen shortly after the crime. Trotsky's guards would have killed him, but the dying revolutionary insisted that he be spared to give details of the death plot.*

Below *Death of a revolutionary.*

on the orders of the NKVD, since he had originally said he had acted as a disenchanted Trotskyist.

What finally upset his story, and the legend that he was a Soviet agent especially hired for the assassination, came after he was sentenced to twenty years imprisonment. He had already been in custody for two years and eight months and it was another year before he learnt that his appeal had been rejected. Those who had interrogated him and put to him the psychological test had never been able to give an accurate version of just who he was. They had found that he was not Belgian, had not been to schools and universities, had not been in the Belgian Army, and the address he gave as a suburban home was in fact the address of a central Brussels store. His name, moreover, was that of a Belgian sports journalist.

It was a drawing which finally gave the clue. He had been asked to draw a plan of a small house with a room for a father, a mother and a son. The man who pretended to be Belgian wrote into the room-spaces the appropriate words, '*mama*', '*papa*', and '*ninoi*', this last word in Catalan dialect, for those room occupants, and in another place wrote '*mama, papa i ninoi*'. Only a Catalan could have written that answer, an answer which sent Mexican investigators to Spain and to Barcelona to establish beyond doubt that Jacques Mornard was in fact Ramon Mercader.

Postscript

The final act to clarify his Sovietisation—if any was needed—came from his own mother, who, disenchanted with Soviet life, and believing that Trotskyists might kill her son, decided to return to Mexico to engineer his release. When she arrived she discovered that other forces, probably Soviet agents, were also planning his release. Rightly or wrongly, Caridad believed that the Soviet Union feared that either of them would discuss Soviet secrets. Caridad had secrets. She had been to Moscow, had discovered that the socialist paradise was not what she had so readily assumed, and was now reasonably free in Mexico. Ramon had no such secrets, and he, too, may have become disenchanted. The Soviet Union had every reason not to want both mother and son destroying the 1940 image of their heroism. Every attempt Ramon made to be paroled was stopped. Every attempt to 'spring' him from jail was fore-stalled. Every attempt to stop his mother from communicating with him was successful. She certainly reached the Mexican capital in the year before he was due to be released, 1959; but at the Lecumberri Prison she was denied a visiting order.

The last that was heard of her was in Paris where she lived close to her married daughter in privacy and disillusionment, known by a different name, and with only the attention of the police surveillance to disturb her in her dotage. As for Ramon, he chose not to rejoin his mother when he was eventually released in 1960. He went to live in Prague, Czechoslovakia. There, he could be living still.

ARCHDUKE FERDINAND~ THE ROAD TO WAR

Europe, at the beginning of the 20th century, was a hot-bed of political activity. Everywhere there was conflict between the new democratic awareness and the old ruling order. At the same time, the urge to expand frontiers, to conquer new lands, to monopolise trade and resources, was causing massive international enmity. This was the backcloth to World War One. It needed just one assassination to spark off that conflagration.

Closest to the actual flashpoint were the people who, despite mutinies, warfare and public murders, had still not achieved independence—the people of Bosnia and Herzegovena, in the Balkans. These territories had been annexed by the Austro-Hungarian empire of the Habsburgs, while neighbouring Serbia remained uneasily independent. There was always the fear that the Empire would expand again to their territory, but what was more likely to cause perpetual trouble was that the Serbo-

Archduke Ferdinand, heir presumptive to the Austrian Empire, occupied the most dangerous seat in power politics. He ruled in the perpetual shadow of a possible World War.

Croat peoples lived in all these three territories and had a common bond of origin and language, a bond which abstract frontiers and political ideals could not break.

On all sides of these frontiers were people who still believed in the unknown Serb who sprang from the dead in 'the field of blackbirds' on Kosovo plain and assassinated the Turkish invader. They were against, even if they were not powerful enough to be united against, the Habsburg Empire. They shared the feelings of hatred against the Habsburgs from schooldays, and it was their emotions which were involved in what happened outside Moritz Schiller's delicatessen on the corner of the Appel Quay and Franz Josef Street, in Sarajevo on June 28, 1914.

Despotic Rule

Those actively engaged in that operation were Bosnians who envied the independence of the Serbians and the efficiency of the Serbian secret society, Ukedinjenje ili Smrt, which had been set up as the direct result of Austria's 1908 annexation of Bosnia. At the head of this organisation was Colonel Dragutin Dimitrijevic, who was known by the code name, and later his nickname, Colonel Apis. The Colonel had been a key figure in the 1903 assassination of King Alexander and Queen Draga of Serbia. Alexander was of the Obrenovic family, for a long time challenged by the Karadjordjevic dynasty, and in addition, he and his wife were, to the population at large, despots.

At the turn of the century, Serbia was watching east and west. Alexander's marriage to Draga, the widowed lady-in-waiting to his mother, and seven years older than himself, was resented by his father. So the father was banished to Austria where the Emperor Franz Josef welcomed him and gave him sanctuary. Alexander, not surprisingly, turned to Russia. He had succeeded in making enemies on either side.

This husband and wife team of Alexander and Draga turned Serbia into an autocracy, she by ostentatiously acquiring wealth while the people became poorer, and he by oppressing the people and punishing those who protested at the excesses which his wife practised.

While villages and buildings were named after Draga, and she appointed her relatives to high positions in the State and in the Army, the soldiers —charged with keeping order—went without food and pay. When the crowds demonstrated against Draga's brother being proclaimed heir-apparent, police were ordered to open fire and arrest ringleaders.

It was as a result of the killing and wounding of many people and the arrest of certain Army officers that a military plot was devised. On June 11, 1903, more than two dozen Army officers with their units surrounded the Palace, blew open the doors with explosives, and searched the royal suites. During the search Colonel Apis was wounded by a bodyguard and held his own revolver to his head, ready to commit suicide should the plot fail. Eventually, a senior officer of the guard showed the intruders a secret room behind the royal bathroom, where the King and Queen hid. The royal couple promptly promised reforms, but their officers emptied their pistols into the pair and then drew their sabres to mutilate the royal bodies before flinging them from the windows into the courtyard below, to the cry: 'The tyrants are no more.'

Colonel Apis survived, even as a regicide, to serve Serbia under the heirs-apparent, first Prince Djordje, then Prince Alexander, and finally King Petar. Despite advice, notably from outside the kingdom, none of them had the inclination or were able to rid themselves of the regicides who were still prominent in official circles. While the Regents wanted to be the sole arbiters of the kingdom's political future, Colonel Apis, supporting the Radical party, wanted Bosnia and Herzegovina to be merged with Serbia. The annexation of these two territories by the Austro-Hungarian Empire made him all the more an opponent of the Habsburg eagle. And it was against this background that a group of young Bosnians anxious to be free of the Habsburgs, sought the help of his secret society in Belgrade in 1914.

A Nation Divided

Emperor Franz Josef, meanwhile, administered his empire as if by divine right, and with a political acumen for ruling diverse nations on this principle:

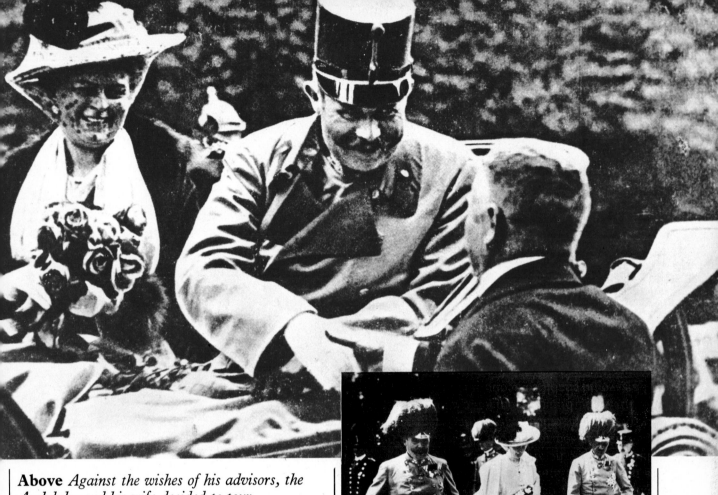

Above *Against the wishes of his advisors, the Archduke and his wife decided to tour Sarajevo in an open car.*

Inset *The visit to Sarajevo, hot-bed of nationalist feeling, was meant to allay the unrest which threatened the Austrian Empire.*

they are of different origins, different ambitions and hate each other. Therefore the empire can have a lasting peace by setting each of them to watch his neighbour, in a state of mutual suspicion and mistrust.

The Emperor was now, however, nearing the end of his life. Born 84 years previously, he had named his eldest nephew Franz Ferdinand, in accordance with the rules of succession as heir-presumptive to the titles of Emperor of Austria, King of Bohemia, and Aposotolic King of Hungary, *et cetera*. He was an able heir, and his only transgression was to marry Countess Sophie Chotek von Chotkowa und Wognin, who came from a family of aristocratic descent which was, in the eyes of the reigning house, low and impoverished aristocracy. With that disadvantage he had to announce his

marriage as a morganatic one, in which his wife and any children of the marriage would be deprived of all rights, titles, privileges and successions. They had a daughter and two sons when the fateful year arrived. Franz was 50 and the Countess Sophie 46. The fourteen years of marriage had been happy and successful, and while there was no suggestion that their heirs could ever inherit the imperial position, the Countess Sophie was a resolute figure by his side. So resolute that it was she who insisted on accompanying him, when the suggestion was made that he should visit Bosnia to watch army manoeuvres. As Inspector-General of the empire's

armed forces, it was unthinkable that he could or would refuse. The question that arose was what precautions were or should have been taken to protect the person of the heir-apparent in a turbulent and notably hostile province?

That such precautions were necessary must have been obvious to the advisers of the Emperor and of the heir-apparent. After all, the Emperor had lived through more than eight decades to see those closest to him die of violent deaths. His only son, the Crown Prince Rudolf, took his own life at Mayerling, a country-house near Vienna, in a suicide pact with Marie-Vetsera, his mistress. The Emperor's wife, Elizabeth, was murdered by an Italian anarchist at Geneva in 1897. His brother Maximilian, who became Emperor of Mexico, was captured and shot by Mexican forces in 1867. And now his closest surviving male relative and the heir to the Empire, was to visit Bosnia and Herzegovina. The Emperor had visited the provinces two years after the annexation and knew full well, afterwards, that he had walked in danger of his life. He had walked as his heir was to walk, among the Serbs who still talked of the defeat of 1389, when the Turks decided the future of Serbia for more than 500 years. That defeat was at Kosovo, and Kosovo became a first name, a Christian name, a name that appeared in poetry, song and folklore, and was used in everyday conversation which turned on Serbian nationalism. Anything which furthered the cause of Serbian nationalism (according to some) could be carried out in the name of Kosovo.

There was a man, Bogdan Zerajdic, the 23-year-old son of a free peasant, who believed this. With this belief he set out to see the Emperor visit the annexed Bosnia in 1911. He borrowed a revolver from a student and saw the Emperor pass between the double ranks of armed guards, but Zerajdic did not shoot. He wrote that he had meant to kill as Brutus had done, but he was overcome by sorrow that Sarajevo, damned and bowing to the Emperor, was a blasphemy against history. That was on June 3. Twelve days later, Zerajdic took his revolver again, and at the door of the Sabor (parliament) he fired five shots at General Marijan

Left *The fatal moment. Gavrilo Princip fires at the royal couple, killing the Archduke and fatally injuring his wife.*

Varesanin, Governor of the two provinces. Thinking that he had killed the Governor, he shot himself dead. Varesanin survived. Zerajdic's last words were, 'I leave my revenge to Serbdom'; and the fact that the authorities gave him a hidden, unmarked grave was enough to ensure that he would be a hero.

Student Conspiracy

Despite all this, the very same day, June 15, *Vidovan*, or St Vitus's Day, was chosen four years later for the visit of the heir-apparent, Archduke Franz Ferdinand. It was a memorable day for a memorial, and the youth of Bosnia were to note it. They had found Zerajdic's grave and had decorated it, but in their minds were other positive acts of violence.

It is impossible to know how many patriots were bent on violence. There were certainly several active groups, groups of three, who used the word *troikas* to describe their revolutionary cells. Two of these *troikas* were to be very prominent in the events of June, 1914. In one of them was a student of nineteen, Gavrilo Princip, whose family were serfs from the Grahovo Valley which separated Bosnia from Dalmatia, a wild, remote gap between the mountains. For years they had been the serfs of the Ottoman Empire, and if they looked for other sovereignty they could choose between the Republic of Venice and the Habsburg Empire which bordered their land. They were poor, and like many of the mountain serfs, had rebelled against the Turks, who raped their women, exacted penal taxes and tributes, and defiled their Eastern Orthodox Christian Churches. Their rebellion came through guerilla bands which could hold the mountains but never the towns below, while the Turks, far from the base of their empire could not hope to vanquish the mountain folk.

Princip had jet-black hair, sharp features and a sallow complexion, but what people noticed, whether they were his friends, enemies, or the examining judge, were his eyes, blue, bright blue, piercing without being offensive. They were apparently all-seeing and were indicative of his intelligence.

He was an able but not an outstanding student, but his book knowledge, covering vast numbers of

Above *Armed police and soldiers hustle away one of the conspirators.*

tomes in Serbo-Croat literature, and, in the translation, socialist, anarchist and revolutionary writers, was immense. His behaviour was correct enough. While he would demonstrate ostentatiously by eating meat during an Eastern Orthodox fast, and by ignoring the Austrian Empire flags and songs, his personal behaviour was monastic. As a revolutionary, he believed that he should abstain from drinking, nor should be associate with girls.

At Tusla High School, where he was a student before transferring to Sarajevo, he met Vaso Cubrilovic, who tended to regard Princip as a maverick, a restless lad, always looking for a goal but never sure where it was to be found. Cubrilovic may have been right, for although only sixteen he was a principal conspirator in what was to follow. But the two closest to Princip were Nedeljko Cabrinovic, eighteen-year-old son of a cafe proprietor, and Trifko Grabez, another school-friend who had been expelled.

In the sping of 1914 these three were all at school in Belgrade, the capital of Serbia, when the news bulletin of the Archduke's planned visit reached them in a plain envelope, sent via the City Hall at Sarajevo, so as to evade the eyes of the censors. After receiving the news, Cabrinovic accepted Princip's offer to meet him at the park where, on a park bench he accepted his invitation to join him in the assassination. And they agreed that Princip's room-mate, Grabez should be the third. The three of them joined a secret society Smrt ili Zivot (Death or Life), which had a Council of Spirits, namely seven people who were pledged to avenge the Serbian defeat at Kosovo 500 years previously. This organisation had two principal rules: membership was restricted to Serbs of Bosnia and Herzegovina and to people of good behaviour who did not touch alcohol. Through this organisation the *troika* obtained four revolvers and six bombs.

They were provided by the secret society of Colonel Apis. Moreover, this society helped them to cross the Serbian border back into Bosnia with those armaments.

They had the support of another *troika* consisting of Danilo Ilic, an older student-teacher who bridged the gap of generations between Bosnian revolutionaries, and who had first taken young Princip to his home as a student lodger years before; Cvetko Popovic, and another eighteen-year-old. Ilic had acted as a mediator between the first trio and the secret society helpers in Belgrade (although it was later suggested that Ilic's job had been to stop the assassination).

Cabrinovic had a row with his father, who wanted to fly the Austrian flag—black and yellow with the black eagle—from his home for the Archduke's visit. So the lad divided up his money between a devoted grandmother and his sister and went into the town where he had his photograph taken 'for posterity'. He then met Grabez and Ilic in a cake-shop, where Princip joined them. Princip handed Cabrinovic a bomb and cyanide poison in a paper wrapper to enable him to commit suicide after the incident. Ilic had already given Grabez a bomb and a revolver, and Princip himself was similarly equipped.

Cubrilovic and Popovic were also out on the Appel Quai that morning for the visit of the Archduke and Duchess.

The Fateful Day

The day began for the royal couple at the Hotel Bosnia, at the Spa of Ilidze. The Archduke had attended the manoeuvres of the 15th and 16th Army Corps in the mountains south-west of Sarajevo, while the Duchess had visited schools and convents. Now they would attend mass at their hotel, be received at the local town hall, and then go on a sightseeing tour of the Bosnian capital, Sarajevo. There would be lunch at the Governor's Palace, a visit to the Museum, the beautiful mosque and the Army inspectorate headquarters.

The Duchess, who had insisted on making the visit at her husband's side, rebuked a politician who had suggested that they should cancel the visit. The Duke was the very essence of calmness. And to cap their contented bliss, a message was delivered to them that Maximilian, their eldest child, now thirteen, had passed his school examinations. On that note the Duke and Duchess set out for Sarajevo.

Appel Quai was then a long street with houses on one side overlooking the low embankment of the River Miljacka on the other. The procession en route for the town hall had passed Austrian flags mingled with the red-and-yellow emblems of Bosnia, pictures of the Archduke, and cries of 'Long may he live.' It was 10.10 am when Cabrinovic, the one conspirator thought to be lacking nerve and courage by his colleagues, asked a policeman to indicate which car the Archduke was travelling in. With that he took his grenade, knocked the pin out on a lamp-post and hurled it at the car. The driver, seeing the flying object, accelerated, and the grenade bounced off the folding canopy at the rear and exploded under the front wheels of the car behind. When the Archduke reached the town hall, not surprisingly enraged, he found that the other cars were not following, and

Below *Police photographs of some of the conspirators. Of those arrested, few survived their heavy prison sentences.*

dispatched an aide to find out what was happening. While he counted the injured, the Lord Mayor of Sarajevo gave the Archduke a flowery greeting which was so embarrassing in the circumstances that the heir-apparent had to interrupt him.

Only when the stuttering welcome finished did the Archduke recover his composure sufficiently to thank the town for its unshakeable loyalty and 'joy at the failure of the attempt at assassination.' He even added felicitations in the Serbo-Croat tongue to show his 'unchangeable grace and kindness.'

Death in the Morning

The grenade thrower had hurled himself into the River Miljacka, which in summer was almost dried up, and he was promptly captured and arrested, as were many bystanders. Meanwhile, the Archduke enquired whether 'more attempts are going to be made against me today?' To which the various replies were taken to be abject apologies and heartening prophesies. The procession would, therefore, continue. The return from the town hall to the governor's residence for luncheon would have involved joining the Appel Quai once again, then crossing the river. The Archduke though, on

hearing that a colonel in his entourage had been hurt in the grenade attack, insisted on visiting him in hospital. And this involved driving the length of the Quai once again.

Now the driver of the car took the wrong turning. Instead of continuing along the Quai, the driver turned right from the embankment, away from the river and into Franz Josef Street. 'Stop!' cried the Governor, and he was about to give the driver new directions when Gavrilo Princip pulled out his Browning revolver. The first attempt at assassination had failed, but by chance the car, in taking the wrong turning had stopped exactly outside the delicatessen of Moritz Schiller, where Princip stood. A policeman tried to knock the revolver from his hand, but claimed that another conspirator intervened, and Princip fired two shots. He had to

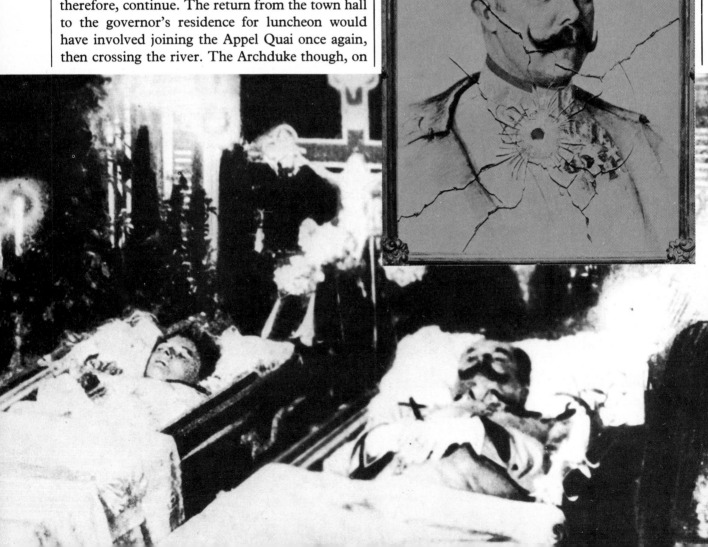

fire across the Duchess as she sat at the Archduke's right side, but the first shot went through the side of the car, and entered her body through her corset. The second bullet fired higher, went right through the high collar·of the Archduke's uniform, smashed through the jugular vein and lodged in the spine.

The Duchess cried out to the Archduke, 'For God's sake what has happened to you?' and sank to her knees, her head in her husband's lap. In that position the Archduke cradled her head and said: 'Soferl, Soferl, don't die. Live for my children.'

A count ran forward to help the Archduke, asking him whether he was in great pain, but the Archduke replied twice, 'It is nothing, it is nothing.'

Their bodies, still adorned with amulets to protect them from evil, were taken to the Konak, the secluded, walled Governor's residence, a relic from Ottoman times, where they were pronounced dead. Both assassination attempts and the deaths had taken place within 90 minutes. It was still half-an-hour before noon as the bells began to toll in mourning.

Arrest and Retribution

Many were arrested. Some were hanged. Only the youth of the principal conspirators saved them from the gallows, although of these thirteen only five ever survived the dungeons.

Cabrinovic, the first to act, was pulled out of the riverbed and taken bleeding from his injuries, some caused in the fall, some by blows, and although he took the cyanide given to him, it merely damaged his mouth so that he could not eat for days. He told his accusers that he was a radical anarchist who wanted to bring down the regime so that a liberal one could replace it. And he, like Princip, and some of the fellow conspirators claimed, in order to protect others, that they were acting on their own.

Left *Archduke Ferdinand and his wife lie in state after the assassination.*

Inset *The death of Ferdinand shattered any hope of a united Europe. Germany was quick to sieze an opportunity to march to war.*

Princip told the examining judge that he regretted killing the Duchess, but that he had acted alone in the assassination. Unfortunately, the stories of the conspirators did not tally and the police were already rounding up Serbs who had been in contact with, knew or aided the principal assassins.

Although there were tight security precautions before the Archduke's visit, covering frontier traffic and student behaviour, the conspirators carried out their tasks with apparent ease. Their journey from Belgrade was devious, and while the police checked main-line stations the students used less noticeable stops. Since registration of new arrivals at the police station was compulsory, Gavrilo Princip obeyed the law and declared that he was staying with Ilic. As a result Ilic was arrested.

Grabez too, had been arrested and tortured, but revealed nothing and it was at this stage that Princip, who had claimed that he acted alone, asked to be confronted with the conspirators. To them he said: 'Confess everything, how we got the bombs, how we travelled and in what society we were, so that just people do not come to harm.' In the interrogation that followed, some of the accused told more than Princip had intended. He wanted only six conspirators named, the two *troikas* that were actually willing to carry out the act of assassination, and not those who supported them in spirit. But not only Cubrilovic and Popovic were arrested.

There were 25 people who stood trial between October 12 and October 23, and many of them were only sixteen years old. All the principals in the drama (except Danilo Ilic, 24, and one figure in the shadows, Mehmed Mehmedbasic) were under twenty years of age. Gavrilo Princip was nineteen; Cabrinovic was nineteen; Grabez was eighteen; Popovic eighteen and Cubrilovic seventeen.

Trial and Verdict

None of their defences tallied in every detail, and the records of the trial which still exist are marked by the fluency of the young defendants. They used the excuses and the reasons of idealism, radicalism, anarchism and socialism in their defences. They quoted from their favourite politico-literary jour-

THE ROAD TO WAR

nals on the principal of assassination being justified if it is against a tyrant, in which case it became tyrannicide. They wanted to kill someone in power in the Austrian Empire—not necessarily the Emperor, not necessarily the Archduke, and certainly not the whole Habsburg family. They wanted the union of Serbs and Croats, a union of South Slavs, and they wanted them united by a new State of Yugoslavia, free from empires and dynasties.

When the hearings were finished, the presiding judge asked all to stand if they were sorry for their part in the assassination. All stood except Gavrilo Princip. Asked why he did not stand he replied: 'I feel sorry for the children who have lost their father and mother. I feel sorry for assassinating the Duchess Sophie because she was a Czech. I had no intention of killing her. That bullet was intended for the Governor of the Province. I do not feel sorry for killing the Archduke, because I wanted to kill him for the reasons I have stated.'

After five days' deliberation, the judges announced the verdicts. Of the accused, all chained in pairs, they sentenced Ilic to death by hanging, Princip received 20 years with hard labour, a fast once a month and a hard bed in a darkened cell on the 28th day of each month, a sentence that was also given to Cabrinovic and Grabez. Cubrilovic received a sixteen-year sentence and Popovic a thirteen-year imprisonment. Thus, older people who took a smaller part in the affair were sent to the gallows, while the young Bosnians, who were the most active, were sent to prison. For most it was a living death. Of the principals, only Cubrilovic and Popovic came out alive. Cabrinovic and Grabez died of tuberculosis and malnutrition within two years. Princip, who fired the fatal shots, lost first an arm and then his life through tuberculosis. When he died on April 28, 1918, the end of the Habsburg empire was only a few months away.

The Consequences

Of such events is history made. It was not a classic assassination by itself; it was neither well planned nor well executed. It had a specific cause but without hope of a worthy result. Its very incompleteness has given armchair commentators field-days in suggesting that the plot was originated by the Germans, Russians, English freemasons and many others. Even when satisfied that it was a Serbian plot, they have dredged the files to hazard a theory that it was the work of Serbs who had emigrated to the USA, a hot-bed of anarchism.

The events of Sarajevo were really only complicated by the war which engulfed the world immediately afterwards. That would have taken place in any case. Whether the actual declarations of hostilities would have followed the pattern which they did is doubtful, but the Germans would have found a reason or an excuse for marching to war. The simpler rather than the complicated facts about the assassination are the ones that matter; that young Bosnians were brought up to believe and know that they had a national entity and a national pride which was put under the Ottoman yoke 500 years before at Kosovo, and in more recent times—although Serbia was a kingdom—by the Austro-Hungarian Empire's annexation of Bosnia and Herzegovina. When Gavrilo Princip killed the Archduke, the Austrians demanded of the Serbian Government ten guarantees. They were designed to punish those who had helped the assassins and to prevent propaganda or other acts against the Empire. The Serbian Government, exhausted by wars, anxious to maintain its sovereignty, agreed to nine of the guarantees, but refused 'a judicial inquiry against those implicated in the murder, and to allow delegates of Austria-Hungary to take part in this.' The Serbian Government, though, was willing to accept a ruling on the point from an International Court at The Hague, or by the great powers which drew up the Serbian Government's declaration of status in 1909. The reason was that it would be a violation of the Serbian Constitution and of the laws of criminal procedure. Despite this reasonable reply, Austria-Hungary declared war on Serbia on July 28, just one month after the assassination. Within seven days all European powers were involved in the bloody conflict which ensued. Gavrilo Princip and his conspirators lived to see something of these hostilities. They did not live to see part of what they fought for—the creation of a Yugoslavia.

Right *Epitaph. The death of Ferdinand did nothing to further the cause of independence for the Balkans or peace in Europe.*

PERCEVAL~ MURDER, NOT ASSASSINATION

To Britons, assassination is a foreign word, a foreign act. It is carried out by foreigners against foreigners. It is a word only used by Britons when discussing the act in another part of the world. Historians of Britain, even when faced with incontrovertible facts of a domestic assassination, prefer to call it murder. Murder is murder, and that is that. Contemporary commentators regard the word as taboo. And if, God forbid, the reigning Sovereign of Britain were to be shot, they would find a way of describing the act which did not involve using such a prohibited word. They are pathetically like elderly ladies at a tea-party who whisper the dreaded initials, 'T.B.', even though that scourge has been almost eradicated, and mothers who in front of their children spell out the letters 'S-E-X'.

It is true that British history is by no means peppered with assassinations, and there are still doubts about some of the most famous murders which come into this category. There is ample scope, within the modern trend, to dredge some of the mysterious deaths of kings and princes to find positive explanations of assassinations. Who can be certain that Rufus, son of William the Conqueror, who was killed by a 'stray' arrow while hunting the New Forest, was not assassinated?

However, there is no arguing that one important Briton—a Prime Minister and First Lord of the Treasury—was assassinated as recently as the 19th century. Mr Spencer Perceval was actually shot in the lobby of the House of Commons, Westminster, at 5.15 pm on May 11, 1812. There were at that time many reasons why an assassin might kill any Prime Minister and more than one reason why an assassin might want to kill Mr Perceval, but the reasons turned out to be somewhat different from those expected.

A Man of Talents

Spencer Perceval came of the aristocracy, a Tory but not a tremendously wealthy man. Second son of John, second Earl of Egmont, he was born on November 1 1762, in his parents' house in fashionable Audley Square, Mayfair, London. He went first to Harrow and then to Trinity College, Cambridge, where he won the declamation prize and graduated with a Master of Arts degree. He had little enough money as a second son and chose to follow a career in law, being called to the Bar at Lincoln's Inn in 1786. He began by practising in the Midland circuit, where his colleague and frequent opponent in the courts, Sir Samuel

Spencer Perceval. Something of a maverick in 19th century politics, this Prime Minister provoked hostility in high places.

Romilly, became his friend. Sir Samuel, a great legal reformer, wrote in his *Memoirs* about Perceval. He found the future Premier, 'with very little reading, of a conversation barren of instruction, and with strong and invincible prejudices on many subjects. Yet by his excellent temper, his engaging manners, and his sprightly conversation, he was the delight of all who knew him.'

Perceval's entry into politics came when Warren Hastings, the first Governor General of India, resigned and returned to England to face a seven-year trial before the House of Lords, over his administration of the East India Company under its Act of Parliament. Murder, robbery, extortion, and hiring out troops to make war were among the 'high crimes and misdemeanours' of which he was acquitted. William Pitt, the Prime Minister, was not in favour of the trial, and his attention was drawn to an anonymous pamphlet which was published on how the constitutional issues involved might be solved. The author was Perceval, and he was congratulated.

Perceval obtained, successively, a large number of Crown briefs including those against Tom Paine, the Whig and Quaker who wrote *The Rights of Man,* and his friend, Horne Tooke, for supporting the French Revolution. He became counsel for the Board of the Admiralty, and the number of silks was increased to include him as a K.C. In addition, Pitt wanted him to become Chief Secretary of Ireland. This was refused for a very good reason—entirely financial. He had married, moved from lodgings in Bedford Row, Bloomsbury, but with money settled on his wife, he moved into a house in Lincoln's Inn Fields. He needed the house to maintain his family, for by 1796 a sixth child had been born and he felt he could not maintain the family's standard of living on a ministerial salary. He did not refuse a Parliamentary seat though, which was found for him at Northampton. His role in the House of Commons was the defender of Pitt, but he reserved the right to oppose Pitt and anyone else on the subject of Catholic Emancipation. Since the Reformation, Catholics had been disbarred from holding political, civil and other offices. Many professions and even trades were closed to them, and it was 1829 before those restrictions were lifted. At the end of the 18th and beginning of the 19th century, though, Perceval claimed conscientiously that sudden relief from the restrictions would result in social and political evils. Those places disbarred to Catholics might overnight be flooded with them.

Political Conflict

At the same time as he conducted his political arguments, Perceval continued at the Bar. Under Mr Henry Addington, later Viscount Sidmouth, he accepted first the post of Solicitor-General and then Attorney-General, but continued to earn from his private practice.

His advocacy in the courts was matched only by his debating powers in the Commons, and although Addington's administration was weak, it was defended single-handedly by Perceval against the powerful opposition of Pitt and Fox.

Perceval, for a time, appeared as the most liberal of Tories, save for his one prejudice—no emancipation for the Catholics. He even refused to prosecute the earliest trade unionists on the grounds that this would give uniform and wholehearted support to the employers in whatever decisions, rightly or wrongly, they made against their employees. Wilberforce's campaign against slavery in Guinea received support from Perceval.

Below *John Bellingham – a man twisted by an irrational grudge against Perceval.*

Above *Ten days before Perceval was assassinated, a Cornishman, John Williams, had a dream in which he saw the Prime Minister murdered.*

The expansionist policies of Napoleon, and the failure of the peace, brought Pitt back, and again, although Pitt had opposed Perceval's remaining in office, he sought Perceval's services—as did the following Prime Minister's, Grenville and the Duke of Portland. Perceval appears as something of a 'Vicar of Bray' within the ever-divided Tory Party, but whatever was offered him, he put financial considerations high on his list of priorities. While Attorney-General, he continued in private practice at the Bar, and when he was eventually persuaded to become Chancellor of the Exchequer, he had to be offered the Duchy of Lancaster as well, to give him additional income. He was also the personal patron of patronage, putting his own supporters onto allegedly independent committees on expenditure. At the same time he had clashed with the Prince of Wales.

An Enemy at Court

'Prinny' was to become Regent when George III fell insanely ill. In 1806, when Parliament carried out its prosecution and persecution of Princess Caroline of Brunswick, whom the Prince had put away, Perceval had taken her part legally and politically. When the Duke of Portland fell ill and Perceval succeeded as Prime Minister in 1809, he had to deal more directly with the Prince. Fox had held that on the illness of the King, the Prince was entitled to become the Regent automatically. Pitt had held that he could become Regent only with a Parliamentary vote. Perceval took the same view as Pitt, and even favoured restrictions on the powers of the Regent. This led to a barely disguised hostility between the Prince and the Premier.

It was not helped by the fact that the Prince was a profligate, had led a debauched life and was, because of his grossly immoral life, scarcely more fit to govern than his insane father; while the Premier was a pious man, a student of the scriptures, and a regular churchgoer. It was made even more difficult because, even though the Princess had been virtually exiled, she had lived a grossly licentious life abroad which had resulted in Parliament carrying out the useless trial against her. Now, in 1810, when the King became ill again, and the Prince was to become Regent, Perceval produced a measure entrusting the royal household and custody of the King's person, not to the Regent, but to the Queen. The Prince made up his mind: he would prepare a new list of ministers so that when he actually became Regent he would have them nominated and exclude Perceval.

But the King was not to die yet.

Spencer Perceval had no real opposition outside his own Cabinet, and such was his personality, his powers of persuasion, and debating ability that he often appeared as a virtual one-man government, prosecuting the Peninsular War. He out-ma-noeuvred those who would 'sell' the Government to the Prince, and defended the handing out of sinecure posts (including one to his own brother, Lord Arden). He had sufficient enemies and sufficiently strong prejudices to produce enemies. His enemies were the Catholics—particularly the Irish—the extreme reformers of the day, the French and, at home, the Regent. He was a prime target for an assassin; it would take only one man with a sense of grievance to shatter the powerful world he had built up. That man existed.

Vision of Death

The curious circumstances were these: On May 1, 1812, a Mr John Williams, of Scorrier House, near Redruth, in Cornwall, told his friends and relatives that he had had a strange nightmarish dream on three successive nights, and each night the dream was precisely the same. The scene he described was clearly identified as the House of Commons, and the lobby inside it. In the lobby, a person in a snuff-coloured coat with yellow metal buttons, drew out a pistol and shot dead a small man in a blue coat with a white waistcoat.

Williams told his story again and again, and could not be faulted in the details. He was discouraged from travelling to London, though. He thought he should warn the authorities, but his incredulous wife and friends dissuaded him on the grounds that, after all, it was only a dream and the important people in the capital city would only laugh at him for his trouble. Besides, who was the man in the dream in the snuff-coloured coat, and who was the man in blue? If he did not know who they were, how could he warn anyone of the trouble he foresaw while he was asleep? Williams was persuaded to remain at home.

At that time in London, there was a man, John Bellingham, who had travelled on business in Russia, where, during the course of his work, he had been arrested by the Tzarist police, imprisoned, lost money and business, and had returned home an embittered man. In St Petersburg he had complained to the Ambassador and to the Consul-General, but without success, and on reaching London he had written to numerous people for redress, including the Prime Minister. The answer he had been given was that what happened in Russia was a result of his own behaviour—offending the laws of Russia—and H.M. Government could not intervene.

That is why Bellingham went to the House of Commons on the afternoon of May 11, 1812. The Prime Minister was under attack that afternoon in the Chamber. His use of Orders in Council, rather than properly voted measures, to pursue the Peninsular War, and raise money for its conduct, had brought violent criticism. They were ruining English commerce, and the manufacturing districts were dispatching shoals of petitions to Parliament against the Orders. Lord Brougham called for an inquiry, and on that spring afternoon the House went into Committee to examine witnesses, when his Lordship protested that the Prime Minister was not present.

An urgent message was sent to Downing Street, and Spencer Perceval, a thin, pale and short man in a blue coat and white waistcoat, walked through the lobby of the House to the Chamber to hear the criticisms against him. As he did so, John Bellingham, in a snuff-coloured coat with yellow metal buttons, stepped out from behind a pillar, raised his pistol and fired at point-blank range, the ball hitting the Prime Minister's left side. Perceval died in the Speaker's chambers before a doctor could be found, while Bellingham was arrested and taken

Right *The Prime Minister lies dying and a shocked Britain is confronted with the grim spectre of assassination in its most hallowed institution – the Houses of Parliament.*

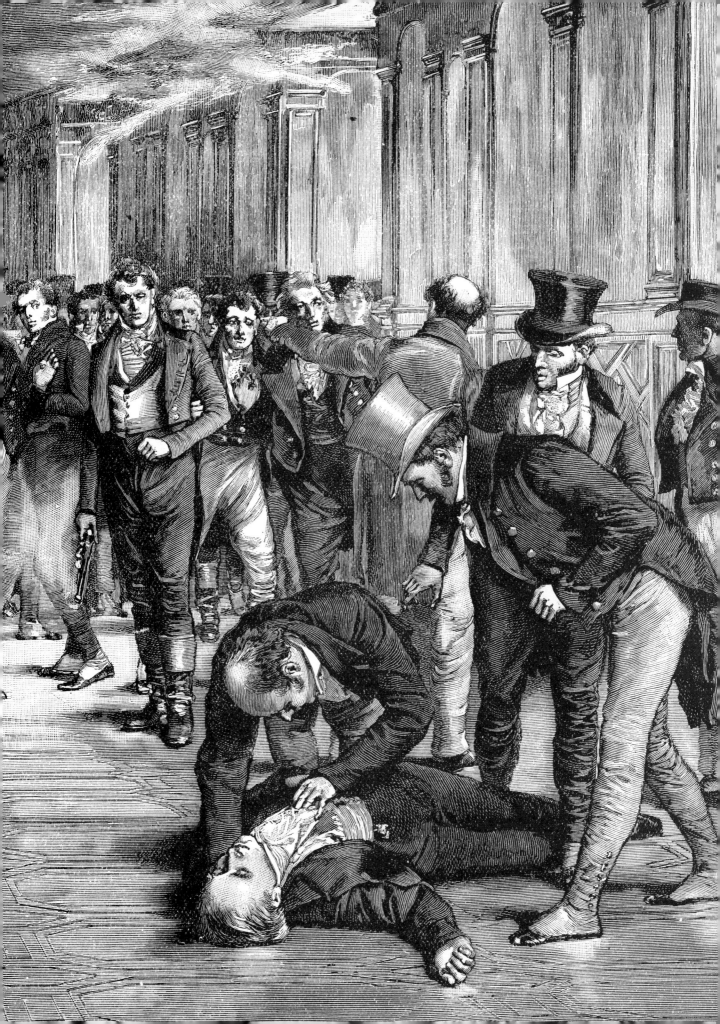

to the cells of the Palace of Westminster. After someone asked the crowd which assembled: 'Where is the villain who fired?' Bellingham stepped forward and said, 'I am the unfortunate man.'

Swift Justice

The name Bellingham being an old Irish settler's name brought the immediate charge of conspiracy, and allegations of others in the House being guilty of complicity, which Bellingham denied. In the House of Lords, the Lord Chancellor wanted all

Below *Thirty years after Perceval's death, an assassin made legal history: Daniel McNaughton, killer of Sir Robert Peel's private secretary, was judged guilty of the crime, but insane.*

the members to remain within the Palace of Westminster until they were sure it was safe for them to venture abroad.

Bellingham was mentally unbalanced, and his resentment over what happened in Russia, plus Britain's refusal to help him, had turned to insanity. 'My name is Bellingham. It's a private injury. I know what I have done. It was a denial of justice on the part of the Government,' was his answer to those who arrested him.

For Spencer Perceval, who died at the age of 49, Parliament voted a monument in Westminster Abbey; but what about his family—his widow, six sons and six daughters? The Prince of Wales, whether through latent generosity, a sense of extravagance or a ploy to win more power for his Regency, asked the Commons to look after the family. They voted £50,000 for the children, £2,000 a year for the widow and for the head of the family after her death, which would first go to the eldest son, then a university graduate, who would himself receive £1,000 a year. On the death of his mother this would rise to £3,000.

Very little has been recorded about Perceval, the virtually unknown but in some ways extraordinary Prime Minister who was assassinated. One is more likely to hear the name of Bellingham mentioned—a most unusual happening in cases of assassination—for Bellingham was to have his name written in the law books. Lawyers anxious to have criminal insanity defined, referred to the case of Bellingham, for at the Old Bailey trial, Sir James Mansfield argued that the criterion for criminal responsibility in mental disease was this: Did the prisoner have, at the time of committing the offence, a sufficient degree of capacity to distinguish between good and evil? Bellingham's plea of insanity was, on these grounds, set aside and he was sentenced to hang for murder.

The speed of justice was amazing. The assassination took place on the evening of May 11, the Old Bailey trial ended on May 15, and he was hanged at the Old Bailey three days later, on May 18.

A Leading Trial

Bellingham's case brought the whole attention of eminent jurists throughout the world to the prob-

Above *Until McNaughton's trial, insanity was not a legitimate defence. The verdict gave a new definition to the term 'criminal responsibility'.*

lem of determining the exact definition of criminal responsibility. Eventually, three decades later, English justice gave the world the definition in the McNaughton Rules. Although they have constantly been criticized, they have held good for many years. Daniel McNaughton, a mad Scotsman, shot and killed Mr Drummond, private secretary to Sir Robert Peel, the Prime Minister. When McNaughton appeared before the courts, his counsel secured his acquittal. He argued the doctrine of partial insanity. The Chief Justice, who sat with two other judges, told the jury that the test was whether McNaughton was capable of distinguishing right from wrong with respect to the act with which he was now charged. McNaughton was insane and therefore not guilty of murder. The judges were questioned by the House of Lords on the ruling, and the McNaughton Rules came into being: knowledge and the nature of criminal responsibility. Knowledge of the nature and quality of the particular criminal act at the time of its commission is the test of criminal responsibility. Delusion is a valid plea for exoneration, when, and only when, the fancies of the insane person, if they had been facts, would have been so. Thus it took two assassinations in Britain to give the McNaughton Rules to the law for interpretation in many, many cases both in Britain and America, not to mention other countries.

HITLER~ BOMB PLOT AGAINST THE TYRANT

World War Two, with its oppression of weak peoples, rather than its battlefield of conflicts, bred new assassins. They emerged as would-be heroes. And they failed more often than they succeeded, for assassination in time of war, when everyone is looking for the proverbial bullet with his name on it, is more difficult to achieve.

The most ambitious attempts at assassination during the 1939–1945 hostilities were the numerous attempts at assassination on the life of Adolf Hitler. They numbered more than a dozen, and all were abortive.

The tyranny of Hitler began long before September 1939. In 1938, four years after he came to power as Chancellor of Germany, while he was actually threatening President Beneš of Czechoslovakia, a group of Army officers were planning a *coup d'etat*, which might have ended in his death if other officers had not reduced the plan to the mere delivery of a memorandum.

After the start of the war, and knowing Hitler's preconceived views of expanding the conflict, the same generals conspired to remove Hitler again. They included General Ludwig Beck, former Chief of Staff; Dr Carl Goerdeler, former German Ambassador in Rome; Colonel Hans Oster, of counter-intelligence, the *Abwehr*; and General Georg Thomas, head of war economy and armaments office. With them, at least in spirit, were two senior men, Field Marshal Walther von Brauchitsch, current Commander-in-Chief of the Army, and General Franz Halder, current Chief-of-Staff.

These two decided to approach Hitler, not with a *fait accompli*, but by using reasonable and plausible arguments, to try to persuade him that the German Army was not then so superior that it could take on the future enemy. They knew that he was

A study in tyranny. Hitler used assassination as a means to climb to power, but he was to find that it was a double-edged weapon.

gambling on quick victory, about which they were more than cautious. They believed he would involve Germany in a full-scale World War. Hitler believed he could pretend that the Allies were waiting to attack Germany, while at the same time he overran another country. The Field Marshal and the General believed that they could pretend they were pointing out immediate difficulties of re-equipping the Army and moving it from Warsaw to France, while they were at the same time waiting for the General Staff *putsch*. The result was that Hitler lost his temper, named the date of the attack in the West as November 12, and although this had to be postponed five days beforehand, and even after that, the *putsch* was abandoned. The Field Marshal and the General welcomed the delay—they knew that the German Army in Poland could not be refitted to cross Europe as quickly as Hitler planned—and they therefore dropped out of the plan to replace Hitler.

The Fuehrer, only a month before his planned attack in the West, which was cancelled because of bad weather forecasts, answered his apparently unknown enemy within, with this national directive: 'Everything is determined by the fact that the moment is favourable now; in six months time it may not be so any more. As the last factor, I must in all modesty name my own person as being irreplaceable. Neither a military, nor a civil person could replace me. Assassination attempts may be repeated. I am convinced of my powers of intellect and decision. Time is working for our adversaries. Now there is a relationship of forces in our favour which can never be more propitious. My decision is unchangeable. I shall attack France and England at the most favourable and quickest moment. Breach of the neutrality of Belgium and Holland is meaningless. No one will question that when we have won.'

First Bomb Plot

While he was speaking, the next and most specific attempt on his life was being planned. He was to speak on November 8, 1939—and every November 8 as long as he lived or could attend—at the Burgerbrau Keller in Munich, the scene of the 1923 putsch which had helped him on his way to

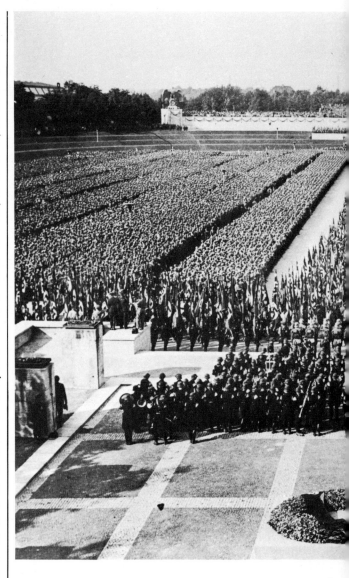

power. There, to the singing of '*Deutschland uber Alles*', and clinking of beer steins, the men of the Nazi Party who had supported Hitler in the early days, could relive their glories of politicking, demonstrating, Jew-baiting and street-fighting at an anniversary party in the place where it all started. He arrived, made his speech, rather shorter than usual, and left to the adulatory chorus of *Sieg Heil*. Soon after he boarded the train bound for Berlin, an explosion rocked the beer cellar, killed several party officials and injured many more.

Dr Paul Joseph Goebbel's propaganda machine could announce that the saviour of Nazi Germany had been saved again. When Hitler heard the news, as his train stopped only 94 miles away at Nuremburg, he was ready to announce, 'Now I am

Above *Mass rallies could not disguise the widespread German opposition to the Nazis.*

to his plans even in high places, and unsure how great the opposition had become, had asked the Gestapo to organise a phoney attempt on his life. George Elser, the carpenter, was chosen from the ranks of victims in Dachau concentration camp to do the work. He had been sent there for re-education in the Nazi way of life, and was told that his life would be spared if he would install the timed explosive in the beer cellar. As a skilled cabinet maker he had no difficulty with the work, and he was taken to the cellar twice nightly before the rally to carry it out. He cut away the panelling of the pillar nearest to the dais from which Hitler would speak, and placed an alarm clock with the explosive inside the recess. Having done so, he was given further instructions about his movements, but he did not return to the cellar to see the fuse attached to the electric current which would be necessary to explode the device. Instead, on the night of the attempted 'assassination', Elser was directed to the Swiss frontier and, as he attempted to cross, he was arrested, complete with a marked photograph of the interior of the cellar and the pillar.

Even an amateur assassin would hardly carry such a document with him, and it is doubtful whether the Gestapo ploy fooled anyone of intelligence. Certainly many, many people must have wondered why, with three such magnificent arrests—Elser was a Communist, the Gestapo claimed—all effected within such a short time, and including one suspect with the evidence on him, there was never any trial, even for propaganda purposes.

Anti~Hitler Factions

Who would really attempt to assassinate Hitler, whose boasts of conquest during the war came true, confounding the generals' assessments? One particular attempt was that of one of Hitler's own chosen ministers, Albert Speer, the Minister for Armaments Production. After a long illness, he returned to his Ministry in June, 1944 and became disenchanted with Hitler's conduct of the War. He steadily came to realise in the next few months that, with the reverses on the Russian and Italian fronts, plus the June 6 D-Day invasion of France, there could be only one result—the defeat of Germany.

content! The fact that I left the Burgerbrau earlier than usual is corroboration of Providence's intention to allow me to reach my goal.' Radio and newspaper bulletins could add that, simultaneously that same night, the Gestapo had arrested, on the Dutch-German and the Swiss-German frontiers, those who had perpetrated the assassination attempt on the Fuehrer. The reported fact that two British Secret Service men had been held on the Dutch border, well over 300 miles away, while a carpenter was arrested on the Swiss border, turned out to be a feeble piece of propaganda.

It is thought that Hitler, knowing of opposition

Hitler, as he saw it, could only live and win. Speer saw quite clearly that Hitler would die, and Germany would face disastrous defeat. But in the months that he planned, there were other anti-Hitler factions at work . . .

Not all might have attempted assassination, since many of Hitler's opponents were practising Christians and pacifists, while many others had the military means but not the opportunity, nor the ability, nor the courage to do so.

While the anti-Hitler activities of the Churches and the Army were independent of one another, there was the one notable attempt of rebellion in which the famous Dietrich Bonhoeffer, former pastor of the Protestant German Church in London, was aided by conspirators in the *Abwehr* to meet the Bishop of Chichester in Sweden, early in the war. The Count Helmuth von Moltke, who died for his beliefs, led the circle from Kreisau in Upper Silesia where many more intellectuals and church folk, of various denominations, met in opposition to the Fuehrer. It was really after Moltke's death—since he did not agree with assassination—that his followers lent their support to the more militant elements, including the Army.

Although the dictatorship of Nazi Germany was virtually complete, the remnants of freedom which threatened the Fuehrer were the Churches and the old Army. The Army was responsible for more attempts on Hitler's life than any other group.

When Pastor Bonhoeffer and others were arrested in 1943, it was because their activities had been traced back to the Army. That was the year in which the hard-core of senior Army officer rebels were to cement their allegiance. General Ludwig Beck had been in the 1938 conspiracy; General Friedrich Olbricht, Reserve Army Chief-of-Staff, had shown sympathy and found an able recruit among his staff in Colonel Graf von Stauffenberg, who had been badly wounded while fighting with Rommel in the Desert. In the East, General Henning von Tresckow, Central Army Group, and his adjutant, Fabian von Schlabrendorff, had found ample reason to join the opposition of the senior staff to the Fuehrer. General Olbricht's second general staff officer, Lieutenant-Colonel Herber, was admitted to the circle, while the old 1938 opponents, ex-diplomat Hassell, and former oberburgermeister Goerdeler were again active in support.

Operation Valkyrie

Stauffenberg, the most courageous of the group, who at 37 held out a metal right arm in greeting—a reminder of his fighting with Rommel's 10th Panzer Division in the desert—was persuaded to believe that Hitler's death could only come about with active political civilian support, and it had been suggested to him that contact with the Communists was the best method. There was an inevitable dispute; and Beck, Goerdeler, Hassell and the Generals involved all favoured an approach to the West. The case for the former argument was that there was supposed to be a Communist underground, while there was not an active Western underground easy to contact. While they bickered, Stauffenberg had persuaded two Social Democrats, Julius Leber and Adolf Reichwein, to make contact with the German Communist groups.

On June 6, the Allies launched the invasion of Normandy. Rommel had warned that the Allies would be out of that limited area and would overrun France in three weeks. Tresckow, in the East, had signalled that his troops could not stop the Soviet offensive. In central Italy, Kesselring sounded a similar call: Retreat! But as the conspirators moved, so did the Gestapo, with orders first to arrest Reichwein and Leber, and a few days later to take in Goerdeler. Both factions, except for Stauffenberg, had been suspected. He was to have three 'dates' on which to end the life of the Fuehrer, all within nine days. On those three occasions, Hitler's life, the length of the War, and the future of Germany depended on the contents and efficacy of the Colonel's brief-case. It contained a dirty shirt, a slab of plastic high explosive and a ten-minute fuse. When this fuse was fractured it released an acid which, in ten minutes, would eat through a wire holding back the tightly sprung striker which, in turn, would detonate the cap of the bomb.

With the bomb was a pair of pliers with which to fracture the fuse. Every single person who knew of the conspiracy was given a copy of the sealed

Right *Colonel Graf von Stauffenberg – war hero and would-be assassin. Like many German aristocrats he loathed Hitler's policies.*

Above *The conference room after the explosion. Only the flimsiness of the structure saved Hitler and his entourage from certain death.*

Left *Hitler explains his miraculous escape to his ally, Mussolini.*

plans of what was to happen if the bomb killed Hitler. It was called Operation Valkyrie, after the mythological Scandinavian maidens who rode through the air, mounted on swift horses, with sword in hand to determine the course of battlefield strife. In intention it was well named. In effect it was still a myth.

On July 11, Colonel Stauffenberg attended a conference ordered by Hitler at Berchtesgaden, his Haus Wachenfeld, the villa 100 miles from Munich on the Obersalzberg, amid the breath-taking scenery of the Bavarian Alps and not far

from the Austrian frontier. After travelling all that way, the Colonel saw Hitler but found Himmler and Goering absent. He decided to wait for another opportunity.

His next chance came on July 15, when Fuehrer Hitler summoned his military commanders to his secret 'wolf's lair'—a forest hideaway at Rastenberg, in the depths of East Prussia. This time Hitler was called elsewhere, cancelled the summons at the last moment, and then a few days later renewed the summons to the same headquarters for July 20. This would be another, and the last opportunity for the conspirators to succeed. It was an auspicious day.

A Miraculous Escape

Stauffenberg had just been appointed Chief of Staff of the Reserve Army and was being summoned to report on the creation of new front line divisions. His appointment was for 12.30pm. Although he did not know it, Signor Mussolini was due to visit the Fuehrer there at the same place that same afternoon. Hitler looked forward to the meeting on that hot summer's day, for he felt safer at Rastenberg since, while at Berchtesgaden, two of Germany's V-bombs had exploded by accident near his home. In the Prussian forest there would be no such worry. He would listen to his military advisers and decide how the war on two fronts was to be continued. He was also forced to make another important decision—to hold the conference in the wooden *Gastebaracke*, instead of in the concrete bunker, where alterations were being carried out.

Stauffenberg, his right metal arm clutching the deadly briefcase, and a black patch over his sightless eye, had put up with a considerable amount of banter over his two previous trips with the briefcase. This time he knew that there would be no mistake. A duplicate bomb was placed in the briefcase of his own adjutant, which would be handy should his own fail to explode. With that added safeguard, the Colonel and the adjutant boarded their Junkers aircraft for the three-hour flight to Rastenberg, followed by the long drive in an Army staff Mercedes to the 'wolf's lair'. Through many check points, via minefields that needed expert navigation, pill-boxes and electrified fences, they were driven to the centre of Hitler's forest hideout. Now for Hitler. But first they had to report to his executive Chief of Combined Staff, the recently appointed Field Marshall Wilhelm Keitel.

Stauffenberg removed his cap and holster-belt as he gave a résumé of the report he would give to the Fuehrer on the difficulty of providing new front-line divisions from the Army Reserve. As the Field Marshal escorted Stauffenberg to the wooden hut where Hitler was to hold his conference, the Colonel apologised: he had forgotten to pick up his cap and belt. Back in the Field Marshal's ante-room, he flicked open the briefcase, snapped the fuse with the pliers and hurried on to the conference room.

The Field Marshal even offered to carry the Colonel's briefcase because of his disabled arm, but the offer was refused. They walked under the aerial camouflage netting to the conference room where Hitler was hearing the first of six reports, the first on the Eastern Front. Keitel presented Stauffenberg to Hitler. On Hitler's left stood Keitel and General Alfred Jodl, on his right Colonel Brandt, next to whom Stauffenberg took his place. The Colonel put down his briefcase and, having already started the fuse, told an aide that he would give his report to Hitler after taking a telephone call from Berlin. Only a minute or two later, at 12.50pm, the acid was through the wire and the striker exploded the bomb with a deafening report. Windows, walls and the roof were all blown out, exposing the guest-house to the elements. Some of

the debris which fell caught fire and guards rushed in as the guarded staggered out.

If they had been in the concrete underground shelter all would have been killed, but because the conference was held in the wooden building, the blast found a ready escape route. There were several dead and injured but there were many survivors. Stauffenberg, leaving the buildings with his adjutant, told another conspirator, General Erich Fellgiebel, Chief German Army signals officer: 'There goes Hitler on a stretcher. We got him this time.' Stauffenberg asked the General to phone the information to Berlin, while he and his adjutant set off in the Mercedes for the airfield. However, Hitler had staggered out of the conference room with a number of injuries, but he was still very much alive. At first it seemed that his clothes had been torn from him by the blast, and he was covered in dust. On further examination

Below *Hitler visiting the injured. He exploited his escape for propaganda purposes.*

A conspirator stands trial. Over 10,000 were implicated in the plot.

doctors found his hair scorched, his back and right arm badly bruised, and an examination showed that both ear drums had been affected. There were to be other effects, not readily discernible, which were to become apparent later.

Stauffenberg's Bluff

Even then, the smile of fortune was on the conspirators rather than on Hitler. He and his aides had thought that the explosion was due to the dropping of a single high-explosive bomb from an aeroplane which, had it struck the concrete bunker would have hardly dented it. While the remaining members of the General Staff conference were returning to Berlin, confident that their assassination attempt had been successful, it fell to the senior signaller, General Fellgiebel, to inform Berlin that Hitler was dead, and secondly to destroy all communications under his command at the 'wolf's lair' so that a counter-coup could not be attempted.

Stauffenberg was confident that this was being done as he headed for Berlin. The pill-box sentry posts and guarded mine-fields and barbed-wire entanglements all presented temporary halts as the conspirators escaped. Guards, including their officers, had heard the explosion and hesitated to allow the Mercedes to pass, but the Colonel ordered them in the name of the Fuehrer to let them through immediately. His metal arm and rows of medal-ribbons, plus his commanding voice, demanded that all barriers be opened. So successful was he in bluffing his way out of the fantastically guarded forest, that after the bomb attempt at 12.42pm, the Colonel, and his adjutant who had been dismantling his spare bomb and tossing the parts from the car window, were aboard the Junkers which took off at 1.05pm.

But, Hitler was not dead, and Fellgiebel was not able to send his urgent message to Berlin. Field Marshal Keitel ordered the communications centre to send a message to all fronts that the Fuehrer had not been killed as might have been reported. Fellgiebel decided, on his own initiative, to ignore the Colonel's order. He sent the next message at 1.03pm, just as the Junkers was about to take off, so that no one in Berlin—waiting to carry out Operation Valkyrie—could be certain or not of the truth. For two hours and 40 minutes— the time which elapsed on that plane journey— none of the key conspirators could be positive as to what had happened.

From the Rangsdorf Airport, Berlin, at 3.45pm, Stauffenberg telephoned General Olbricht, and in answer to his questions reported, 'Hitler is dead, General. I saw his corpse carried out.' As a result of that report, Operation Valkyrie went into action, with signals to all fronts telling generals to open their sealed orders, arrest all Nazis and *Schutz Stafeln* (SS) leaders, and take over Germany. In Berlin, General Beck and Field Marshal Erwin von Witzleben were ordered to take over the War Ministry in the Bendelstrasse, while Major Otto Remer, commanding the elite Berlin Guard Battalion, was told that the SS had attempted to overthrow Hitler, killed him, and he should arrest Dr Goebbels who had been a party to the plot. In Paris, Nazi leaders were being arrested in large numbers.

Major Remer was persuaded by a political officer attached to his unit, to check the command, and was allowed to speak first to Goebbels, and then to Hitler himself at Rastenberg, whereupon he was promptly promoted Colonel by the Fuehrer and ordered to put down the revolt. Hitler himself had recovered sufficiently to welcome Mussolini to his retreat, and in the wrecked conference room told him: 'After my miraculous escape from death today, I am more than ever convinced that it is my fate to bring our common enterprise to a successful conclusion.' Later, Hitler ranted and raged and declared: 'I have been chosen by Providence to make history, and all those who try to thwart me will be destroyed. I shall be revenged upon them all.'

Hitler's Revenge

Fortune should have still been with the conspirators since Fellgiebel, after sending his message, should still have carried out his instructions to wreck the communications centre at Hitler's headquarters. This would have enabled Operation Valkyrie to supersede and take priority over Field Marshal Keitel's command to tell the world that the

Fuehrer was alive and well and in charge at Rastenberg. But Fellgiebel was among the first to be disillusioned. Not only had the new Colonel Remer been able to telephone the 'wolf's lair', but when Stauffenberg reported to General Fritz Fromm at the War Ministry that Hitler was dead, the suspicious General challenged the truth of the statement, put in a call to the 'wolf's lair' and heard Keitel declare angrily, 'Yes an attempt was made on the Fuehrer's life, but he is still alive and not seriously hurt.' And, he added, 'When Stauffenberg arrives, place him under arrest until further notice.'

When Fromm announced that Hitler was alive, and the conspirators were under arrest, they promptly disarmed him, put him in custody, and put General Erich Hoepner in charge as Commander-in-Chief of the Reserve Army. Colonel Remer, however, was on his way. Fromm was released, and Olbricht, Stauffenberg and Haeften were marched out into the courtyard of the Ministry. With their backs to the wall, facing the glare of lights from the guards' armoured cars, they were executed by a firing squad. Olbricht congratulated the one-armed Colonel who shrugged his shoulders, leaving on the flagged yard his last message—the heavy clank of his metal arm as he died. His adjutant died praying.

The revenge of Hitler was to be terrible. Investigations, executions—with or without trial—and court hearings into the July 20 plot were to continue until the very last day of the war, ten months later. Von Witzleben, General Paul von Hase, General Hoepner and General Helmuth Stieff were all sentenced to slow hanging. The families of Goerdeler, Stauffenberg and Hassell were arrested; many more were sent to concentration camps. A moderate estimate suggests that 4,980 were actually executed, and many more thousands sent to the camps as a direct result of the abortive assassination attempt, although many of the victims had little or absolutely nothing to do with the conspiracy.

Rommel Implicated

There is no doubt, now, that Field Marshal Erwin Rommel, the most popular and most able of German commanders, was linked with the conspirators. He had been in contact with Beck (who, incidentally, was permitted to shoot himself) and Goerdeler, but because he had been injured when his car was hit by British fighter aircraft, he was unable to advise, let alone take part. He was for the most part unconscious when Paris heard the news of the attempted assassination. General Heinrich von Stulpnagel, Military Governor of France, and General Hans Speidel, Chief of Staff, Army Group 'B', carried out their orders and imprisoned Nazi and SS leaders. Field Marshal Gunther von Kluge, who had the whole command of the German forces in that theatre—and like the ill-fated General Fromm, who challenged Stauffenberg on what had happened—decided to wait for confirmation before allying himself with the conspirators. When news reached Paris, von Kluge sided with the Fuehrer. Fromm, like von Kluge and many more senior officers, all knew of the conspiracy but waited to see whether Providence stayed with, or turned from, their Fuehrer before deciding how to act. Ironically, Fromm was eventually court-martialled for cowardice, and executed anyway.

When Hitler was convinced that Rommel was among those who had conspired, he gave his favourite commander the option of facing a People's Court or committing suicide. For the sake of his family, Rommel took his own life, but Hitler—unable and unwilling to tell the world that this great Field Marshal had turned against him—ordered him a State funeral at which Field Marshal Karl Rudolf Gerd von Runstedt represented the Fuehrer. This Field Marshal declared that Rommel had died as a result of an accident and added: 'His heart belong to the Fuehrer.'

Although there were attempts to deny the Army's guilt in the bungled assassination they, like the other armed forces, found themselves being overridden and undermined by the SS which had been ordered to put down the revolt. The revenge on the Army and other armed forces in this way weakened their morale and resolve and slowed the pace at which they would fight for the remnants of Nazi Germany. As they fell back before the advancing forces of the Allies, Adolf Hitler himself began to show the effects of the threat on his life and the increasing opposition within Germany. His hands shook, he lost his temper more often, and

Above *Rommel – the legendary 'desert fox'.
He, too, was implicated in the plot.*

accompanied his conversations and speeches with allegations and threats which became more and more intemperate.

Germany's Destiny

There was to be yet another attempt on his life. Herr Albert Speer, the Armaments Minister, having recovered from his serious illness, became gradually despondent at the demands Hitler's war effort was making on the people, the economy and the nation. As a result, in the early part of 1945, he devised a scheme by which poison gas could be introduced into the ventilation system of Hitler's underground bunker. This plot had to be abandoned for technical reasons and the possibility that the attempt might not be successful. Speer at least tried to thwart Hitler in other ways. He had independence of mind, but like so many top people around Hitler, he believed that Adolf Hitler was Germany's destiny and that Germany could not escape that destiny.

LINCOLN~
THE PRESIDENTIAL RISK

Twenty four days after the assassination, in Dallas, Texas, of President John F. Kennedy of the United States of America, Bill (later Sir William) Connor, columnist 'Cassandra', of the London *Daily Mirror* arrived in Washington and wrote the following perceptive note about assassinations:

I said to the taxi-driver, 'The Lincoln Museum.'
He looked blank.
'You know, the house where Abraham Lincoln was shot.'

Abraham Lincoln occupied the Presidency at a critical period in American history. A civil war and the issue of slavery made him a natural target for the assassin's bullet.

He looked blank.
'The Old Ford Theatre where the President was assassinated.'
He looked blank.
So I navigated to Tenth Street between E and F Streets right in the heart of Washington and we made it.
Thus do fame and tragedy fade—at least in the minds of Washington taxi-drivers.
The old theatre building still stands and the ground floor is

the Lincoln Museum, which contains letters and documents of the great President; paintings, photographs, engravings, statuary and the Derringer pistol with which the actor John Wilkes Booth murdered him.

The museum was empty when I went in. At the far end is a large model of the theatre as it was on the night of April 14, 1865. You press a button and a loud-speaker booms out the melancholy tale.

How the President and his wife went to see Tom Taylor's celebrated comedy *Our American Cousin*; how in the third act the assassin crept into Lincoln's box, barred the door behind him; how he fired his gun and put a bullet into his victim that entered above the left ear and lodged behind the right eye; how Booth leapt from the box, crashed on to the stage twelve feet below him, smashed his ankle and shouted, 'Ever thus to tyrants!' and managed, in spite of his injuries, to escape on horseback; how Mrs Lincoln was overcome with grief and how Booth was shot dead twelve days later by an avenger.

I left the museum with the ghastly parallel of Dallas inevitably in my mind. A gun. A head wound. An escaping assassin. The President's wife right beside him and the killer himself soon struck dead. A nation's tears.

Guns down the years.

What the late Bill Connor wrote then is true forever and it applies not merely to the two assassinations he had in mind, not only to the killing of a total of four US Presidents, but to all assassinations.

Cardinal though the crime of assassination is, it is a permanent, unfortunate pattern of life, imitated *ad infinitum,* punished usually without failure, and forgotten. Forgotten by potential victims and forgotten by potential assassins. Like the Bourbons, 'they have learnt nothing and forgotten nothing'. Just consider the history of assassination—American style—ancient and modern.

A Perpetual Danger

When Abraham Lincoln became the President he sat at his desk in the south-east wing of the White House, overlooking the parkland. Over the mantelpiece to his left hung the indelible likeness engraving of the tough old survivor President Jackson. In a drawer of the huge desk, he had a file marked 'Assassination', and in another had been added the words 'hazarded attempts'. They were neatly labelled in chronological order and numbered 82. On Good Friday, April 14, 1865 hazarded attempt number 83 was to be successful.

Before turning to the theories on this particular crime, Mr Lincoln, the sixteenth President of the United States, had himself given his own version and opinion of at least some of the 82 alleged plots and alleged attempts on his life. So often was he warned about such conspiracies against his person, that the *Washington Chronicle* quoted him as saying, 'The only certain way to eliminate all risk to the person of the President, is to imprison him in an iron box where he cannot be made a target for assassins and he cannot perform his duties to the Union.' To his closest confidantes he spoke more than once on the subject: 'If I live in constant fear of being killed I must die not once but over and over again. . . . If it is God's will that I must die at the hand of an assassin, I must be resigned so to die.' And in his sleep he dreamt of being assassinated.

His somewhat neurotic wife, who sought solace from spiritualism, pestered him with her dreams. He, in turn, dreamt that he walked into the bathroom of the White House where weeping citizens were paying homage to a corpse lying on the catafalque guarded by Union soldiers. 'There seemed to be a death-like stillness about me. "Who is dead in the White House?" I asked one of the soldiers. "The President. He was killed by an assassin," was his answer. Then there came a loud burst of grief from the crowd, which woke me from my dreams. I slept no more that night and, although it was only a dream, I have been strangely annoyed by it ever since.' If he was annoyed, his principal bodyguard, US Marshal Ward Hill Lamon, was petrified.

More often than not, when the Marshal warned of an assassination attempt, the President shrugged it off with a casual answer. On one occasion he told the Marshal, who was frightened of a plot to turn the country into a military dictatorship: 'I do not fear this from the people any more than I fear assassination from an individual.' On another occasion, when a bullet had actually gone through the President's stove-pipe hat, he cast aside the suggestion that it was deliberate, preferring the notion that a householder had discharged his gun accidentally. On yet another occasion he forbade any publicity about a near miss, warning the Marshal: 'I do not want it understood that I share your apprehensions. I never have.' Nevertheless, the President in another discussion with the Marshal delivered a more objective view of assassination. It is worthy of study:

'Why put up the bars when the fence is down all around? If they kill me, the next man will be just as bad for them; and in a country like this, where our habits are simple, and must be, assassination is always possible, and will come if they are determined upon it.'

With this kind of fatalism he went about his business on that fatal Good Friday. With that kind of determination that actor John Wilkes Booth went about his.

The Formative Years

Abraham Lincoln took his name from his grandfather who had been killed in an Indian uprising in 1784, 35 years before the future statesman was born. The family came from Kentucky but

Above *Brother fights against brother at Shiloh. In defeat, the Southern states harboured a deep hatred against the 'Yankee President'.*

wandered to find work, and in a log-hut in Harden, Kentucky, the President-to-be was born to Nancy, wife of Thomas Lincoln. Tom came from a line which originated in Hingham, Norfolk, and whose forbears were among the earliest pioneers. His wife, Nancy Hanks, Abe's mother, had died when he was a boy, and the future President had little more than ten months schooling in his whole life. His father was illiterate—a small, struggling farmer— so his son went to work with his hands.

He loaded, ferried and unloaded cargo on the Mississippi, from Ohio to New Orleans, splitting rails on the new iron roads crossing to the West, lumberjacking and performing other tasks for which his six feet-two inch frame, long, muscular arms and powerful hands were seemingly intended. But Abraham's book learning led him to clerical work, in which he would hire himself out to a millowner, a provisions store, and the post-office. He was looked up to in many respects.

Abe would referee cock-fights, judge horse races, and help settle minor disputes between neighbours. The family had by then moved to Decatur, Illinois, and when 1832 brought the Black Hawk War against the Indians, the neighbours chose Abraham to command a troop of volunteers. When he returned a local hero, he found that he could continue to run the mill and the grocery store where he had once been a part-time clerk, but the neighbours wanted something more for him— namely his services as a Whig (later Republican) representative for New Salem in the Illinois legislature. With the same dedication that he had applied to bring himself from illiteracy to a reasonable educational standard (with the help of *Aesop's Fables,* John Bunyan's *Pilgrim's Progress* and biographies of George Washington and other worthies), he applied himself to law.

He was only 23 when he went to war with the Indians, 25 when he was elected to the legislature, and 27 when, qualified as a lawyer, he rode into Springfield with no money and few possessions, to set up practice. 23 years passed in which he helped build the practice with his partner, before he joined the newly formed Republican Party, the principal aim of which was to stop the extension of slavery in the country. Republican nominee for the post of Vice-President in 1856, he was defeated, but in the next quadrennial election he was the successful nominee for the Presidency.

Already he had said farewell to Springfield and entrained for Washington—a twelve-day, five-state rail journey on which he was to make his views, and those which divided the nation, abundantly clear.

Most of the Southern states had already seceded from the Union and elected their own President, Jefferson Davis when, on February 13 1860, the day after Lincoln's 52nd birthday, he was declared President of the United States. In Cincinnati, New York, Philadelphia, Wilmington and Baltimore, Lincoln pledged himself to peace. He declared himself opposed to slavery but declared that he had no purpose to interfere with slavery where it already existed. That was a law and he had supported it. But while the South feared that the new Republican administration would end slavery, which they regarded as a pillar of their civilization, the North feared that the South would march on Washington in defence of their beliefs.

Below *Negro slaves at work in a Southern cotton field – pawns in a political struggle.*

Right *Study of a President. Lincoln was a true exponent of the American democratic ideal.*

A Nation Divided

So fierce was the controversy that even before Lincoln was installed in office there were fears for his life. He was already sneered at in sophisticated New York circles for being a farmer's son, and the manner in which he disguised himself to slip away from Baltimore and enter Washington brought the charge of cowardice from his opponents.

In little more than a year he was disproving the charge as the Union and the Confederate states went to war, a bloody civil war in which the hand of brother was set against brother, family against family, and eventually, when it was over, the hand of the assassin against the President.

Lincoln, despite the words of many 20th century commentators, did not advocate equality. He wanted to see the end of slavery, but he thought it would come about by colonizing Negroes, which would have become, in fact, a form of 19th century *apartheid*. He was willing to see any number of slaves freed and colonized, but he did not make their freedom the main part of his policy. He wanted, he said, to protect the Union of States, reunite the South with the North, and he wanted to do that, come what may of the slavery question. At the same time, he elevated the slaves by changing his own terminology from niggers to Negroes, then to coloured men, then to intelligent contrabands, and then free Americans of African descent; all extremely laudable improvements, but destined to make the South even more bitter towards the North and more intensely hostile to Lincoln himself.

This was intensified even further by the defeat of the South in the Civil War, and by the fact that in 1863, Lincoln did declare the emancipation of all slaves, an act designed to turn the civil bloodshed into a moral crusade with the hope of ending the conflict. The interference over slavery, the loss of human life in battle, and the bitter gall of defeat did

Below left John Wilkes Booth – matinee idol and assassin. A Southerner, Booth never forgave the Northern states for destroying the union of the South. To Booth, Lincoln was the epitome of Yankee aggression.

Far left Four of Booth's conspirators. From left to right they are : Michael O'Loughlin, Sam Arnold, Samuel Mudd and Edwin Spangler. They all received heavy jail sentences.

Left Mary E. Surratt. She owned the boarding house in Washington where the conspirators met. She was sentenced to death by hanging.

not endear Lincoln to a large section of the population, and certainly not to John Wilkes Booth, a popular, respected actor; handsome and wealthy, an athlete and lover, every inch of him a gallant. His father was Junius Brutus Booth, a tragedian of both the London and the American stage, and his brother, Edwin, older and more experienced, who popularized Shakespeare in US theatres.

Scenario for Assassination

Booth was more than a season's matinee idol. Named after John Wilkes, the English reformer who fought for the liberty of the Press to report Parliamentary proceedings, John the actor was pledged to the so-called right of the South to keep slaves. Before the war he served under Colonel Robert E. Lee, and stood guard when the fanatic John Brown was executed before being left amoulding in his grave. He then turned pacifist and, during the war, was content to continue acting when he was not advocating, in the Northern

territory, the case of the South, privately and clandestinely. His good looks, curly black hair, full moustache, and fur-collared cape, silver-knobbed cane and other theatrical accroutrements, enabled him to charm ladies, while his money enabled him to buy liquor for those whom he wished to impress with his anti-Republican and anti-Lincoln views.

This was done on occasion at Mrs Mary Surratt's small boarding-house on H Street, Washington, where George A. Atzerodt, a Prussian who ferried Northerners to the South and Southerners to the North across the Potomac for money, used to lodge. They would be joined by two of Booth's school-day friends, Sam Arnold and Michael O'Loughlin, at other meeting houses in the city. With them went an idiot, David Herold, who was unemployed because of his practical jokes and lack of concentration. And there was Lewis Paine, a tough soldier who had fought with the Confederates, and could be relied on to kill without compunction or conscience. Captured by Union soldiers and hospitalized, he escaped and decided to remain in the Northern territory to rest from the rigours of war and to seek an easier, less disciplined, but more comfortable way of living.

What they conspired to do has been exhausted by historians and theorists and there is little doubt that, as they practised wrestling, throwing knives, and firing guns without ammunition, they were bent on ending the life of President Lincoln— whether they did it first by kidnapping him and delivering him to Confederate authority in Virginia, or by sudden death in the streets. They were bent on homicidal injury.

Planning and Preparations

Booth, who had intended that Paine should kill the President, changed his mind and charged him with the task of murdering the Vice-President, Secretary of State to the Cabinet, William H. Seward, a venerable white-haired statesman of 63, who was at that moment lying ill, having broken his arm and his jaw in a fall from his carriage. Because Paine was unable to follow his instructions to the letter, Booth assigned to him the services of Herold, who knew Washington well, and who would guide Paine to his victim. Arnold refused to have anything to do with the murder. Atzerodt got drunk, threw away his bowie knife and went on a saloon crawl instead. Booth the actor then went to his final rehearsal for his dramatic act.

He already knew that on that Good Friday, April 14 1864, President and Mrs Lincoln were going to Ford's Theatre to see Tom Taylor's comedy *Our American Cousin*. Originally, it was thought that General Ulysses S. Grant, hero of the Union army, and his wife, would be going too. Booth would have undoubtedly sought the end of both men's lives, but had to be content with one. He hired a powerful mare, went to a billiard saloon, drank brandy and wrote a confession of conspiracy and murder before anything had taken place, and he addressed it to the Editor of the *National Intelligencer*, signing it J. W. Booth, Paine, Atzerodt and Herold. The letter was handed to a friend, still before the great drama, who later read it and tore it up in fear.

Booth then carried out his full rehearsal by drilling a hole through the panelling of the President's box, and arming himself with a piece of pine board which would ensure that when he had entered the box, he could not be followed. The wood, braced between a niche in the wall and the door, would act in place of the lock which had been broken accidentally and never repaired. All this he carried out, having ensured that he was alone in the theatre auditorium and unlikely to be disturbed. And he did so with a precision which was to make assassination by an actor a classic in the annals of the crime.

President and Mrs Lincoln and their guests, Major Henry Rathbone and Miss Clara Harris, his fiancee, arrived at the theatre at 8 pm, when the first act was several minutes old, and which was interrupted while the 1,675 patrons stood and cheered and the orchestra played the patriotic song, *Hail to the Chief*. The Chief, who had suffered from nervous tension throughout the Civil War, and had just been re-elected for a second term, had aged tremendously. His own marriage to Mary Todd Lincoln, a better educated society girl from Kentucky, had been happy, but his preoccupation with matters of state and her jealousy and extravagance had more than soured the match; but here was a moment of diversion. Seeing his guests holding hands, the President took his wife's hand in the semi-darkness of the theatre box, as Laura Keene, a celebrated actress, raised the laughs in the comedy being acted before them.

The Drama is Enacted

Outside, Booth had someone to hold his hired horse, while he, dressed all in black, wearing a false beard, and having touched his eyebrows and moustache with a black pencil, stuck a knife in his waistband and two Colt revolvers in his frockcoat. In his hand, however, he held the really lethal weapon, the six-inch-long Derringer, ornately decorated in silver, and already loaded with a 7/16-inch lead ball, the hammer of the single-shot weapon cocked for action. John F. Parker, one of the President's four bodyguards, had already quit his post outside the box to go for a drink, and Booth was able to watch through his spy-hole for his cue to bring drama to the comedy. It came when Mrs Mount-Chessington, anxiously trying to marry off her daughter to a wealthy American, Asa Trenchard, discovers that he is not wealthy. 'I am aware, Mr Trenchard, that you are not used to the manners of good society, and that alone will excuse the impertinence of which you have been guilty,' she declares as she makes a dramatic exit. To which Trenchard says to himself, 'Don't know the manners of good society, eh? Well, I guess I know

Right *The brooding statue of Lincoln is set against the flag and eagle of the USA – in mute testimony to the power and heavy responsibility of the American Presidency.*

enough to turn you inside out, old gel. You sock-dologizing old mantrap.' At that moment, repeated at every performance, the receptive audience went into convulsions of laughter. At that moment, Booth stepped into the President's box, murmured his immortal but less dramatic words, *Sic semper tyrannis,* and fired the Derringer, the lead ball entering Lincoln's head above the left ear, penetrating the brain and lodging behind the right eye.

Rathbone was already on his feet grappling with Booth, who drew his sheath knife and slashed the major's arm to the bone; then he leaped from the box onto the stage, but caught his new spurs in the curtain as he went. Crashing onto the stage he fractured his left leg just above the ankle; he brushed people aside, felled the lad minding his horse, and rode off heading south.

Flight to the South

The assassination was at 10.15 pm and, as planned, the fellow conspirator, Paine, reached the bedside of Secretary of State Seward, and finding that his Naval Whitney revolver did not fire, he smashed it down on the head of the defenceless son of the statesman who had asked him to wait outside the bedroom door. Inside the room Paine went beserk, slashing at three other occupants and injuring a woman. When he threw his weight behind the knife aimed at the occupant of the bed, the Secretary of State, although slashed about the face, rolled off the bed onto his broken arm, escaping more serious injury. Paine escaped, but not before he had injured six people with his knife. The Secretary of State was to survive the bloody attack by another eight years. He had been saved, perhaps, by the iron brace which held his fractured jaw in place, although he carried for the rest of his days a hideous scar on his right cheek.

While the President was carried from the black walnut, red upholstered rocking chair in the theatre box, to the tailor's across the road, where he was to linger for hours until the following day, Booth, accompanied by Herold, both on horseback, managed to cross the Navy Yard Bridge to the South. Once closely guarded during the Civil War, the pass system had been relaxed; they had little difficulty in heading south to Maryland, seeking refuge among the unsuspecting and the sympathetic, and Booth moving despite his fractured leg. Bound up by a friendly doctor, Booth and his companion continued their 80 mile escape route, recrossing the Potomac into Virginia, crossing the Rappahannock River until they took refuge in a tobacco-drying barn. There, soldiers, unable to persuade Booth and Herold to give themselves up, set fire to the barn. Herold gave Booth his carbine and surrendered and was tied to a tree. Then, as the flames took hold, a single shot rang out in the night. It was 3.15 am, eleven days and five hours after the assassination of the President. The assassin was also dead.

After death comes doubt. Mrs Surratt, who kept the boarding-house, Paine who attacked the Secretary of State, Herold who guided him there, and Atzerodt who just remained drunk (although he asked many questions about the Secretary's whereabouts), were tried, condemned to death and hanged in the Arsenal grounds. O'Loughlin and Arnold, although not directly concerned, were sentenced to hard labour for life. This too was the sentence on Dr Samuel Mudd who dressed Booth's wounded leg on his escape journey. A six year sentence was given to Edward Spangler, a scene-shifter, also alleged to have aided Booth's escape. After conviction comes the quarrel.

Mystery and Doubts

While it has become an American custom to turn events into extravaganzas, it is common to all 'quickie' historians to judge events centuries afterwards by inappropriate standards. The punishments for the prisoners, including the fact that they were hooded and manacled while awaiting trial, are said to be vicious, although justice anywhere in 1865 would seem antiquated by present day standards. Evidence that O'Loughlin was conspiring to kill General Grant, who later became President, has been discounted. But the most fantastic of all theories is that Lincoln's assassination was really plotted by Secretary for War Edwin Stanton, the President's right-hand man during the civil conflict.

He is supposed to have declined the invitation to the theatre on the fatal night, persuaded General

Above *As Lincoln and his wife watch the play being enacted before them, Booth stealthily enters the box. Always an actor, he waits for his cue, mutters the words,* Sic semper tyrannis, *and shoots the President with a Derringer.*

Grant not to go either, and, after the assassination, to have dilly-dallied and misdirected those seeking the assassin as if to allow him to escape. This extravagant allegation is largely based on a discovery by Mr Raymond A. Neff, of Gibbsboro, New Jersey, who bought a second-hand bound volume of Colburn's *United Services Magazine* for July–December 1864, for the price of 50 cents in 1956.

In this book he discovered what purports to be the writings of General Lafayette Baker, head of Stanton's National Detective Police Force. In them, Lafayette is supposed to tell how Stanton planned the assassination and how Lafayette feared for his life. Mr Neff's further researches suggest that Lafayette was murdered by arsenic poison to ensure his silence.

Such doubts mystify perpetually—there are many more too countless to be enumerated. But it is interesting to see, how 100 years after the death of Lincoln, in the aftermath of the infamous slaying of John F. Kennedy, the American people should still prefer mystery and extravagance to a cold, factual judgement.

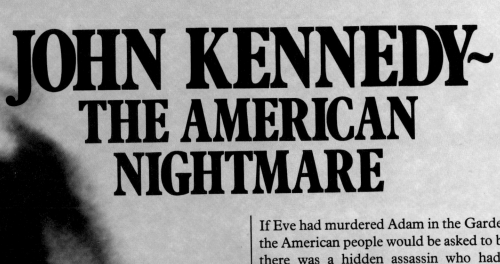

JOHN KENNEDY~ THE AMERICAN NIGHTMARE

If Eve had murdered Adam in the Garden of Eden, the American people would be asked to believe that there was a hidden assassin who had not been brought to justice. Such is the American way of death and its aftermath.

The most outrageous American assassination will for long be regarded as the killing of President John F. Kennedy, at Dallas, Texas, on November 22 1963. His death brought the world to mourning. Yet, before the horror of the murder was forgotten, the world had to be treated not only to more tragedy, but also to the curious theatrical pantomime and circus of the American aftermath.

Basically, the John F. Kennedy assassination facts and chronology are well known and will be repeated here only briefly and when essential. The prosecution case presented on the day after the shooting was that Lee Harvey Oswald, a social misfit who hailed from New York, had taken a rifle to his workplace, the Texas School Book Depository, and from a sixth-floor window shot the President of the United States as he drove in an open motorcade towards a triple underpass.

Oswald, separated from his wife and two-year-old daughter and one-month-old baby, lived in a cheap room in the working-class section of the town. And, after the assassination, he was thought to be returning there when he was challenged by the police; he shot dead Patrolman J. D. Tippitt, and vanished into a cinema where he was cornered and arrested. Two days later, Oswald was being taken from Dallas police headquarters to the county jailhouse, in full view of reporters, photographers, radio and TV teams, when a local strip-club owner, Jack Ruby, aged 52, stepped out of the crowd and, at point-blank range, shot Oswald dead. Those facts are simple enough, but before the assassination of the President had been investigated, before Jack Ruby had stood trial on the charge of murdering Oswald, there arose in America, and overseas, clamorous cries of 'Oswald is Not Guilty' and 'Dallas was not just to Jack Ruby'.

Security Failure

Both cries were made, not unnaturally, in the name of justice. Both cries, in the name of justice, should have been stifled at source. They grew from points of reasonable criticism that, firstly, the President of the United States should not have gone to Dallas because the Texas town housed some elements politically hostile towards him. President Kennedy himself, at the Hotel Texas, Fort Worth, waiting to fly to Dallas, spoke to his wife, Jacqueline (now Mrs Jacqueline Onassis), and to his closest friend and adviser, Mr Kenneth P. O'Donnell, about the role of the Secret Service protecting the President and ensuring that enthusiasm and unruliness did not degenerate into a riot. The President added these words: 'If anybody really wanted to shoot the President of the United States, it's not a very hard job. All that one has to do is get in a high building some day with a telescopic rifle, and there is nothing anybody can do to defend against such an attempt on the President's life.' Two and a half hours later, what the President had said was confirmed.

The Secret Service was, not surprisingly, attacked for failure to prevent the assassination,

WANTED

FOR

TREASON

THIS MAN is wanted for treasonous activities against the United States:

1. Betraying the Constitution (which he swore to uphold):
He is turning the sovereignty of the U.S. over to the communist controlled United Nations.
He is betraying our friends (Cuba, Katanga, Portugal) and befriending our enemies (Russia, Yugoslavia, Poland).
2. He has been WRONG on innumerable issues affecting the security of the U.S (United Nations-Berlin wall-Missle removal - Cuba-Wheat deals-Test Ban Treaty, etc.)

3. He has been lax in enforcing Communist Registration laws.
4. He has given support and encouragement to the Communist inspired racial riots.
5. He has illegally invaded a sovereign State with federal troops.
6. He has consistantly appointed Anti-Christians to Federal office: Upholds the Supreme Court in its Anti-Christian rulings.
Aliens and known Communists abound in Federal offices.
7. He has been caught in fantastic LIES to the American people (including personal ones like his previous marraige and divorce).

although if they had prevented it on this occasion they had the President's logical statement that they could not prevent it for all time. The Federal Bureau of Investigation (FBI) and the Dallas police, knowing that the President was visiting Dallas, were criticised, perhaps reasonably, that they did not check on Oswald's movements that day, especially as he had a record of politically motivated violence. He had shot at an extreme right-wing, anti-Kennedy army officer who had been cashiered from the Army because of his political views. And there was criticism that the Dallas police did not take sufficient security measures to protect Oswald from such a death as was meted out to him in public by Jack Ruby in front of TV and still cameras.

The Arguments

Acceptance of all these criticisms does not by any means excuse the unreasonable and sometimes hysterical outbursts which were already in circulation. The President (the critics were saying) had not been shot from the back, or only from the back; he had not been assassinated by a lone sniper, but by at least two gunmen; Oswald had not acted alone but was part of a conspiracy; Oswald, who had been to Russia, had tried to renounce his American citizenship and affirmed his allegiance to the Soviet Union, would not murder a liberal President, but the southern Texas anti-liberal politicians would do so; Oswald could not have killed the President because his marksmanship was not sufficiently accurate, and he certainly could not have done so without a telescopic sight which his rifle did, or did not, have.

In his favour, Oswald was or had been a Central Intelligence Agency (CIA) agent and an informer for the FBI—or vice-versa—or both. Besides, he had had access to money in the past, even when

Above left *To many Americans, Kennedy's liberal policies smacked of Communist influence.*

Left *Lee Harvey Oswald. A former Communist who had lived in the USSR, he saw in Kennedy the epitome of American imperialism.*

Above *The window from which Kennedy was shot, and the position of the Presidential car.*

unemployed, so why should he not have been in the pay of some conspiratorial organization?

Doubts were cast upon the accuracy of the alleged direction of the fatal gunshots. Doubts were voiced whether Oswald could have fired so accurately, even if the direction was right, and whether he could have reloaded his rifle to fire three rounds so rapidly. The critics have been disturbed that a man who called himself Oswald had appeared at a Dallas firing range for practice but had not been positively identified. The rifleman may have been laying a false trail to incriminate Oswald. Then there is the story that Oswald was an FBI agent, which the FBI has denied, but which the critics keep reiterating, presumably in the hope that it will be confirmed (although many equate 'agent' with 'informer' and could not tell the difference). Recent court reports in America and in London, concerning Americans, show a growing defence habit of claiming on behalf of the accused that they are CIA or FBI agents or informers. Agents are permanent or semi-permanent employees, while an informer can be anyone who helps the authorities. Oswald's educational background and ordinary behaviour did not suggest at any time that he could have been an agent.

Anyone in the case who corrected a statement, withdrew a statement, attempted suicide or was subsequently murdered must, of course, have done all these things or had murder done to him because of the conspiracy. Any suggestion that a witness could have erred and then honestly corrected himself, or been completely mistaken and withdrawn his testimony had to be ignored by this group of critics.

Heritage of Violence

The logic of premise, argument and conclusion was abandoned. The cacophony of criticism continued, with two major voices, unrestrained, incautious, leaving doubts in the minds of those who heard them. These two critics were lawyers, Mr Mark Lane, the New York attorney, who defended Oswald, mostly after his death, and Mr Melvin Belli, the well-known Californian criminal lawyer, who defended Ruby. Before examining their behaviour in the wake of the assassination, it is only right to draw attention to the fact that the USA, despite its century-plus of civilized federal government, still to this day betrays a frontier spirit—a spirit which allows arguments to be settled by firearms. It is part of the national heritage, and any move (as there was in 1968) to limit the ready supply and sale of guns has been met with an equally vociferous move to maintain that sale and supply. Every year 2,000,000 guns are bought in the US; and they go towards 2,600 accidental deaths, 6,500 murders, 10,000 suicides, 44,000 serious assaults, 50,000 robberies and 100,000 non-fatal injuries. And most guns are sold and used in the south, where President Kennedy was killed, as was Dr Martin Luther King, the Negro leader, five years later, and in the west where the late President's brother, Senator Robert Kennedy was assassinated in 1968.

Implicit in the type of government by federal states is the states' independence in making and executing their laws and control procedures. And this might explain some of the hostility shown to the town of Dallas and the State of Texas by visitors from other states, whether they were sightseers, business trippers, newspaper, magazine or television reporting teams, or lawyers. To many of them, Dallas and Texas were foreign parts and, from the start of the Presidential visit, they were going to be treated as such. At the same time Texans, like other inhabitants of the southern states, despite their innate hospitality, have a tendency to treat visitors as foreigners—and especially as damn Yankees.

While these antagonisms were undoubtedly present on the morning of November 22, 1963, they were well below the surface as the Dallas folk prepared to welcome, not a political ally, but the President of the United States. There were voices against his visit, and on that very day a page advertisement appeared in one of the newspapers, attacking the President for his allegedly 'soft' attitude towards Communism and his pouring out of foreign aid to unsympathetic governments. Thus with a bouquet in one hand (cowboy boots for Mrs Kennedy and Texan pony saddles for her children) and the brickbat in the other (the advertisement plus the private feelings of conservative politicians), Dallas welcomed the President.

The Oswald Controversy

Two days later, with the President dead, his assassin dead, and the assassin's murderer awaiting trial, Mr Mark Lane, the left-wing attorney from New York, began a public campaign on behalf of the dead Oswald. The exact hour and date of Mr Lane's appointment as Oswald's defence lawyer is not precisely known, although Mr Lane's supporters have repeatedly complained that Oswald, on his two appearances before Press and Television cameras, asked for legal representation. The Warren Commission report which probed the assassination for President Johnson held that he was not denied the right of legal representation. Whenever Mr Lane was engaged, it must have been between Oswald's first public appeal for legal representation at shortly after midnight, on November 22, and before 11.21 am the following day when Ruby shot Oswald dead. When I asked Mr Lane about this, during his speaking tour of London and other European centres, he told me that he had been retained by the late Mr Oswald's wife, Marguerite. Obviously the defence he had to offer would no longer benefit his client, Lee Harvey Oswald, but Mr Lane persisted in this unusual defence on behalf of a dead man long after the event. He wrote 'Brief for Oswald' in the *National Guardian* news weekly on December 19 1963, which was claimed by one of his supporters to be a monument to free men's determination to seek and tell the truth until the real killer of the President

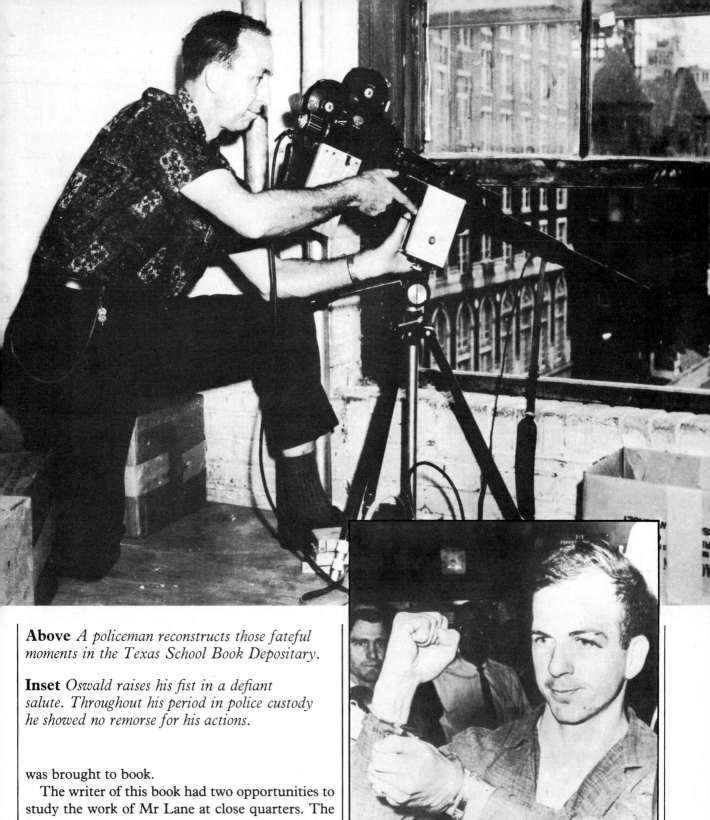

Above *A policeman reconstructs those fateful moments in the Texas School Book Depositary.*

Inset *Oswald raises his fist in a defiant salute. Throughout his period in police custody he showed no remorse for his actions.*

was brought to book.

The writer of this book had two opportunities to study the work of Mr Lane at close quarters. The first was when he addressed a 'Who-killed-the-President?' meeting in London. The London School of Economics had for some reason refused to allow the meeting to take place there, and it was therefore transferred to Red Lion Square, Blooms-bury, a more sympathetic venue for such a meeting.

Mr Lane's lecture was fluent enough; but as far as being a brief for Oswald it was a piece of totally unacceptable pleading. It consisted almost entirely of pointing out the discrepancies between what happened, what witnesses said had happened, what newspapers, magazines, television and radio commentators said had happened. In an unrehearsed sudden crime such as assassination, in a country like the United States, it is not surprising that among the most careful observers, the most meticulous reporters, the most reticent public officials, and the most brash of the entertainment side of that razzamatazz that passes for the American way of life, there should be error and inaccuracy. Nor would it be surprising if more than one officer or official, fearing that his promotion would be blocked or his head would roll, metaphorically speaking, would trim his report to suit his own salvation. But what Mr Lane did was to take every single, solitary discrepancy he could find, check it, often against equally inaccurate reports from rival publications or rival media, and offer that as proof that Oswald did not kill the President and that it must have been somebody else.

The Rumours Spread

What happened next to Mr Lane and the Private Citizens Committee of Inquiry which he founded was even more astonishing. President Johnson had set up the Warren Commission under the chairmanship of Chief Justice Earl Warren to investigate the assassination of President Kennedy, and Mr Lane had asked permission to appear on behalf of his dead client, Oswald, and was at first refused. Later he was allowed to appear in a different capacity.

The Warren Commission, incidentally, largely answered Mr Lane's criticisms when, from a position of safety, they could say: 'The numerous statements, sometimes erroneous, made to the Press by various local law enforcement officials, during this period of confusion and disorder at the police station, would have presented serious obstacles to the obtaining of a fair trial by Oswald.'

At least the Commission had accepted that there were many statements, some of which were erroneous; but Mr Lane was not satisfied. An able

speaker, a former New York Assembly man, he was dubbed as the High Priest of the Plot as he charged two dollars a seat for tickets to attend his illustrated lectures on Who-Killed-Kennedy? He showed with cleverness the discrepancies between different people's stories, but then—like so many of his followers—produced no definite answer to explain these differences. Lawyer Melvin M. Belli, who defended Ruby, appeared with Mark Lane in one of these lectures and he asked the New York City audience whether they thought that witnesses had lied to the Commission because of fear of the FBI, Secret Service, or President Johnson. Incredibly, says Belli, they cried, 'Yes.' On the day the Warren Commission Report was published in Washington, DC (a Sunday), Lord Russell, the distinguished philosopher, called a Press Conference at a public house off Fleet Street, London, to discuss the Report. The famous professor was not himself present, but at his home many miles away. Instead, one of his secretaries and spokesmen, Mr Ralph Schoenman (now barred from Britain and other European countries as a result of his propaganda activities), took the chair to attack the Warren Commission Report on much the same lines as Mr Mark Lane had done on his speaking tour before the Commission had met. It was somewhat disconcerting to listen to views, attributed to Lord Russell, on a Report which occupied so many volumes and which no human being could possibly have read between publication time in Washington DC, and the afternoon Press Conference in London, England. How did this feat of reading and understanding come about? The writer himself had had a copy of the summary of the Warren Commission Report flown to London and had not even completed reading that —at a very fast rate—when the Press Conference began. In answer to the writer's questions, Mr Schoenman confessed that neither Lord Russell nor he had a copy of the Report, but 'Lord Russell has spoken at length on the telephone to Mr Mark Lane.'

There is no doubt that Mr Lane, if he had been able, would have defended Oswald to the best of

Right *Two days after the assassination, as Oswald was being escorted from Dallas police H.Q. Jack Ruby shot him dead.*

his ability, but it would be better to draw a veil over the extra-curricula activities of the Who-Killed-Kennedy? circus.

Dallas on Trial

Mr Melvin M. Belli, the colourful courtroom character, best known for his defences of celebrated Hollywood film stars, was retained to defend Ruby on the charge of killing Oswald, and was paid with a cheque that 'bounced'. Nevertheless, he defended Ruby expertly and in the only way possible —by seeking bail, by seeking a change of venue for the trial, by challenging the maximum number of 900 jurors empanelled, and by objecting to certain contemptuous behaviour in the court precincts. All this was powerful and legitimate, but Mr Belli said or implied throughout the trial that justice in Dallas was not available to his client. Even this was fair play while his client was before the courts, and while he was trying to prove that Ruby had suffered from a form of epilepsy which was shown on the brain charts that had been taken electronically while he was in custody. Where the ploys went beyond the pale, was to perpetuate the charge began by some, fanned by others, and crowned by Mr Belli, that it was really not Oswald who was first charged, not Ruby who was charged with the killing of Oswald, but Dallas, Texas, itself. It was all the fault of a town called Dallas.

Dallas needs no defence. The critics can carp until kingdom come and attack or sneer at Texan customs; that the trial judge chewed tobacco and spat it into a spittoon; that smoking was allowed in court. No one minds the political sniping that Dallas Republicans had been offensive to the late Adlai Stevenson, ambassador to the United Nations, and that while on a visit two local men had spat at him, and the city had apologized. No one minds recalling that Vice-President Lyndon Johnson, as he then was, was besieged in Dallas by Republicans shouting 'Johnson Go Home.'

Stevenson survived the incident, and Johnson insisted that he would still walk his wife across the street to lunch despite the demonstrators, which he did. And what politician worth his mettle could not survive that type of behaviour?

Then there was the charge that Dallas was at fault because her typically southern residents are Protestant, and by nature and upbringing anti-Roman Catholic (Kennedy was one) and anti-Jewish (Ruby was one), so, therefore, how could Dallas sit in judgement on such an issue? The list of charges against Dallas made by Mr Belli and others is formidable. It is said that the American Southerner is the greatest gentleman in the world except for his prejudices. His prejudices, according to one's religious, racial and political beliefs, make him an opponent.

No one in this case—except Dallas and her residents—could be wrong.

The Shattered Hope

The fact remains that the Catholic President of the United States, from Boston, Mass. on a state visit to Dallas was assassinated by a nominal Protestant, Lee Harvey Oswald, a native of New York, who was in turn murdered by Jack Ruby, a Jew from Chicago. Dallas, being a city in Texas, an admitted state of the Union, was a competent venue with a competent judicial authority to deal with the crime or crimes before it.

Whatever the temporary controversies over the assassination, no other conspirators have ever been found, nor have any been named, suspected, interviewed, or suggested. Fortunes have been spent on keeping the controversies alive, but not one cent of that money has produced a satisfactory, solitary fact that would support the contentions of the controversialists.

Students of assassination, like the writer, may find immense satisfaction in sifting and wading through the mountains of documents supporting the various theories, launching the red-herrings, and reaching unacceptable conclusions. It may be sufficiently regrettable to the bulk of the populations of the world to know that President John F. Kennedy, in whom the youth of America and beyond placed their hopes for peaceful prosperity, was assassinated—without pursuing any fantastic dream theories.

Left *Kennedy's death shocked those who saw in him the great hope for a democratic world.*

THE RACIAL MOTIVE

Europeans will find it easier to interpret many assassinations of recent years in terms of racial dispute. This may be true of some but, curiously, not necessarily so in the cases of the major assassinations. There is no doubt, among the minor instances, that Mr Medgar W. Evers, the Negro leader, of Jackson, Tennessee, secretary of the National Association for the Advancement of Coloured Peoples, was killed for racial reasons. President Kennedy had only just finished a broad-

Rioting negroes in Detroit flee before hoses turned on them by the riot squads.

cast when it happened. The President had asked every American to examine his conscience as to why Federal troops had been called in to enforce the law in Alabama. Two fully qualified Negroes had been refused entry to the University of Alabama at Tuscaloosa, and the Federal troops were there to ensure that the Supreme Court's ruling that they had a right of entry was enforced. Evers, in his official capacity, had reason to be proud of his support from the White House in Washington. He did not live to enjoy it. On the doorstep of his home in the neighbouring state of Tennessee he was shot in the back and killed.

That was in 1963, and the racial conflagration which flared up in the United States continued. By 1965, some Negroes, tired of non-violent methods of protest, had adopted the extremism of the original Arab *Fedayeen*, and they called themselves Black Muslims. They preached violence and were behind many acts of terrorism. It followed that violence would be met with violence and, on February 21, 1965, Malcolm X, the anonymous leader of the Black Muslim movement, was shot dead in Manhattan, New York. Two days later a mosque in Harlem, the city's black ghetto, was gutted in a fire started by arsonists.

Even peaceable demonstrations were not safe from violence or assassination. On March 9, at Selma, Alabama, 67 Negro demonstrators were injured. The following day Dr Martin Luther King, the Negro leader and preacher, asked 500 churchmen, clergy and laity, to march to Selma for voters' rights. State troopers halted the marchers at the city boundaries, where the participants knelt in prayer and then dispersed. That night, though, came the violence, when one of the visiting clergy, the Reverend James Reeb, a Unitarian minister from Boston, Massachusetts, was killed—a fate which was to be shared by three other clergymen during August. They were shot in the back during a black-versus-white conflict.

America already had its civil rights laws covering voting, public accommodation, public facilities, public education; it banned discrimination on the grounds of colour in hotels, restaurants, petrol stations, amusement arcades, and publicly owned libraries, golf courses, and swimming pools. But it proved more difficult to enforce the laws than to pass them. Liberalising laws only produced more violence, yet even then there is still a question-

mark over the assassinations of two people in the world who were principally regarded as the apostles of racial separation and racial equality respectively, Dr Hendrik Frensch Verwoerd and Dr Martin Luther King.

Agent of Apartheid

Verwoerd, son of a Dutch missionary, was born in Holland and, like the settlers decades before him, he emigrated to South Africa. He became a professor of applied psychology and at the same time edited the racialist journal the *Transvaaler*. His German education and belief in the mastery of the white peoples led him to support Hitler in World War Two, a philosophy adopted by many Afrikaners. The negative policy of *apartheid*, laughable under the premierships of Malan and Strijdom, became a positive and serious affair under Verwoerd. His way was not to argue about who got to the Cape of Good Hope first, blacks or whites (since neither originated there), but to proceed from the principle that they should not be born of the same parents, live, marry, work or die together.

In this he was more pure and honest than most racialists. South Africa was enjoying an economic boom and *apartheid* was costly. This Prime Minister swept away such criticisms. They would be separated. The blacks, mainly Bantus, had for long been able to come in from the impoverished rural lands, tried to join the economic boom, and got as far as the shanty towns on the edges of the big cities. They were to get no further; and Europeans were even forced to employ Europeans instead of non-Europeans. Verwoerd's plan was to eject the Bantus to 'protected' states where they could elect their own parliaments. While he did set up one of these eight proposed states, his own right-wing extremists protested at the mounting costs of the programme. There were always pressures from the left against *apartheid*, but these were ruthlessly suppressed by an efficient and often over-zealous police force.

It was, perversely, because of his economic policies and not his practise of *apartheid* that he was eventually assassinated.

He had had warnings of unrest. In March, 1960,

Above *Dimitrio Tsafendas. He had a history of mental illness.*

Above right *Dr Hendrik Verwoerd. As the chief architect of apartheid he increasingly drove South Africa into an isolated position.*

a demonstration against the racialist laws at Sharpeville, Johannesburg, turned into a bloodbath in which more than 80 were killed and 250 injured, when police fired on the mob. Three weeks later, in a Johannesburg park, the Premier himself was to be a target. He had just finished haranguing the belligerent white audience with mob-stirring militancy. 'We shall not be killed. We shall fight for our existence,' he declared. He sat down and Mr David Pratt, a local farmer, entered the VIP stand and said quietly, 'Dr Verwoerd?' The Prime Minister turned round and Pratt shot him twice, once in the cheek and once in the ear, before being overpowered.

Pratt was taken to court, and even though he declared, 'I think I was shooting at the epitome of *apartheid*, rather than at Dr Verwoerd,' he was declared mentally unfit to plead against the charge.

The charge was attempted murder, for the Prime Minister unbelievably survived and returned to his work two months later. He appeared again in public with a white dove, which he called a messenger of goodwill, but his message was the same. 'I have known no sleepless nights about the native problem because I know I am right,' he said. The 'winds of change' which Mr Harold Macmillan saw blowing across Africa did not, he thought, affect him, but he was already reaping the whirlwind. South Africa left the Commonwealth and he refused permission for black-controlled states to send black ambassadors to his country. His parliament supported him.

Messenger of Death

Among the messengers who served him in the parliament in Pretoria was Dimitrio Tsafendas, of Greek descent, or so he claimed. A bachelor, fond of languages, fluent in some, a dabbler in others, he could say something in English, German, Greek, Portuguese and Afrikaans. He had been a merchant seaman, had been in mental hospitals, and was fond of quoting the Bible.

He was sufficiently rational to cheat Dr Verwoerd's own racial laws. Born in Mozambique of a mulatto woman and a Greek-Egyptian, he managed to avoid *apartheid*. He persuaded the authorities that he was white, a European, intelligent and suitable for South African citizenship. Even Parliament gave him a post as a messenger; but behind the scenes he was in opposition. That the Government did too much for coloured peoples and not enough for whites was his constant complaint. If they cut the programme for non-Europeans, they could pay him more than $140 per month, he reasoned.

On September 6, 1966, he decided to do something about it. At 11.40am, asked to take a message, he said, 'I have something else to do.' At 12.30pm he told colleagues that he did not feel like eating lunch. Soon afterwards, in his black and green uniform, he walked through the assembled Parliamentary chamber and strode straight up to Verwoerd. The Premier clearly thought that there was a message for him, but the message was death. Tsafendas pulled out a knife and stabbed the Premier repeatedly in the neck and chest. Verwoerd died and Tsafendas was eventually sent to a mental institution.

An attempted assassination and an actual assassination on the same Premier, the arrest of both assailants, and their arraignment resulted in no trial because of the attackers' states of mind. Thus posterity has been robbed of a modern display of how justice would handle the inevitable charge of assassination and the inevitable defence of tyrannicide because of racialism. Immediate posterity was soon to be robbed again when a trial did take place, the trial of the assassin of the American Negro leader and preacher, Dr Martin Luther King.

It may well be that neither South Africa nor the United States of America could withstand such a public and publicised trial, without grave damage to national image and even graver public reaction. In Pretoria it was the psychiatrist who decided it was not possible; in Memphis it was the lawyers. The politicians must have sighed with relief.

Man of Peace

Dr King, clergyman and civil rights leader, was born in racially segregated Atlanta, Georgia, and with his father as co-pastor, he was to succeed his father-in-law as minister of the Ebenezer Baptist Church. No Bible-puncher, he was an educated theologian, abhorred Negro emotionalism in churches and was devoted to practical Christianity. This devotion won him the Nobel Peace Prize in 1964, the third Negro to achieve the honour and, at the age of 35, the youngest peace-maker among the holders. He was the father of the 'sit-in' as a civil disobedience campaign, and his campaigns

for desegregation—before and after the desegregation laws were passed—made him famous. In Montgomery, his second Baptist ministry, and home town, he carried out his greatest works, suffering discrimination, preaching forgiveness, and behaving according to his principles, sufficiently militantly to arouse positive action, sufficiently moderate to be in keeping with Christian love.

He achieved much, but his conservatism was insufficient for the growing militancy of many Negroes, and his progressive influence among leading white peoples invited suspicion and opposition from both races. He preached non-violence, but far too few people could bring themselves to support this Christian ideal in areas of black *v* white violence. Perhaps fewer could accept that the principles of love-your-black-neighbour-as-thyself can be enforced through the statute book. President Kennedy thought it could—and was wrong.

Certainly, very few people would accept either of these principles in Memphis, Tennessee, where the pride and the prejudice of the South is focused. That is no place for evolution, or revolution; but the man who knew no boundaries for his work went there, preached there and was assassinated there. In his last sermon on the mount of intolerance he said: 'Every now and then, I guess we all think realistically about that day when we will be victimized with what is life's final common denominator, that something we call Death. We all think about it, and every now and then I think about my own funeral. And I don't think about it in a morbid sense. And every now and then I ask myself what it is that I would want said, and I leave the word to you this morning. . . . I won't have any money to leave behind. I won't have the fine and luxurious things of life to leave behind. But what I do want to do is to leave a committed life behind, and that is all I want to say.'

That day James Earl Ray, alias Eric Stavro Galt, alias John Willard, alias Harvey Lowmyer, had booked in at a $4-a-night flop-house for the night of April 4, 1968. Ray was not going to sleep there that night. Instead he locked himself in the bathroom and looked out of the window at the balcony of the Lorraine Motel just 205 feet away. When Dr King appeared on that balcony, Ray, using dum-dum bullets in a .30–'06 calibre rifle, fired a single shot and killed the Negro peacemaker.

International Manhunt

Arresting the assassin was no simple matter. He had checked in at the shabby hotel under the name of Willard, bought the rifle with telescopic sight and

Negro marchers pass a hoarding purporting to show Dr King at Communist training school.

Above *By his peaceful championing of civil rights, King did much to advance the Negro cause; but he also made many powerful enemies.*

a box of bullets in the name of Lowmyer, and had driven away in a Ford Mustang car registered in the name of Galt. When the FBI found the car, and subsequently the room rented by Galt, they discovered only one single solitary fingerprint. Despite the seeming impossibility of such a task, the FBI traced that one piece of identification to James Earl Ray. He had a criminal record.

In police jargon he was an all-time loser. Persistent though he was in the field of crime he was a failure, leaving his bankbook at the scene of his first

Above *By his peaceful championing of civil rights, King did much to advance the Negro cause; but he also made many powerful enemies.*

crime, a typewriter robbery, in Los Angeles. Once he fell out of a getaway car after a shop robbery, and in another crime forgot to close the lift doors while trying to dodge a pursuing policeman. A 20 year prison sentence for armed robbery sent him to Missouri State Penitentiary and he was on the run

Above *Robert Kennedy pursued the same policies as his brother – with tragic results.*

from there, after his third escape attempt, when he arrived in Memphis.

The trail from Memphis took detectives to Toronto where Ray, using the name Ramon George Sneyd, had booked in at a dilapidated rooming-house and then left. Royal Canadian Mounted Police had picked up the trail and then discovered that he had, barely two months after the assassination, flown from Toronto to London. Scotland Yard detectives in London picked up the trail, but the quarry had acquired new tickets in London to fly to Lisbon, Portugal.

While Portuguese police reported no trace, detectives permanently stationed at London Airport kept the FBI request in front of them and kept watching. Then, on the night of June 7 and 8, three months after the killing, a detective stopped a newly disembarked passenger and asked for his passport. It showed his name as Sneyd, his nationality Canadian, and the passport had recently been issued in Toronto. From London Airport a call to Detective Chief Superintendent Tommy Butler, chief of the Yard's flying squad, brought him to the airport. Butler, famous by virtue of his capture of

members of the Great Train Robbery gang, took Sneyd to Cannon Row police station, the ancient office off Whitehall.

Sneyd denied that he was anyone else but Sneyd, and in the face of his denials could hardly be detained without further good cause. His identity photographs looked nothing like those circulated by the FBI, and it would be grossly impractical to ask one or more witnesses to fly from the States to London to identify the man being questioned. As time went on, Sneyd was offered a drink of water which he accepted gratefully. No sooner had he put down the glass than it was whipped away, dusted for fingerprints, and a picture of the prints wired to the FBI in Washington. Back came the message. Fingerprints are those of James Earl Ray.

Ray was extradited to stand trial at Memphis, but his trial, which lasted a mere two hours and seventeen minutes, answered none of the agonizing questions. Did he act alone? Or was he the chosen hireling of conspirators? In any case, where did a man on the run get sufficient money for his car, rifle and bullets, passenger trips to Toronto, then London, then Lisbon and the unused tickets for Brussels found on him when he was arrested?

If Ray had pleaded Not Guilty and compelled the prosecution to tell the jury the full story of his assassination, he would have undoubtedly been sentenced to death. But he pleaded Guilty, the story was not told, and the jury did not have to decide the issue of Guilt or (as they do in the United States of America) the sentence. As a result he received from the judge the sentence of 99 years imprisonment, and, for what that is worth, his life was spared.

Circle of Hate

It is not sufficient for the victim of an assassination, political figure though he may be, to have entered office and committed his name to any act. He can be merely a successor to a policymaker, or an adherent, and may not be even that. Robert F. Kennedy, younger brother of the assassinated John F. Kennedy was assassinated during the preliminary campaigning for the presidency of the United States. He was seeking the Democratic Party nomination for the candidature of that office in Los Angeles, California. The very application to the democratic peoples of that city in that state brought him the now all too-familiar death blow of the bullet. And the full reasons tend to be lost once again in the psychiatric circle of suspicion.

He was one of the four original sons of Joseph F. Kennedy, the former Ambassador to London, the father of ambition. John, the second son was assassinated, so was his younger brother Robert, leaving the youngest boy, Edward, to cope with his political future. Robert undoubtedly hoped to follow in his brother's footsteps, not merely to the White House, but in the fashionable liberalism of the Democratic Party. It was still a very live, attractive, vote-appealing programme of equal rights, desegregation of races, removal of urban poverty and powers to fight growing crime. None of this should have brought Robert Kennedy more than the normal potential violence. But he was a victim of a different kind of power-group: racialism.

His assassin was a remote, but not remotely controlled protagonist. Sirhan Bishara Sirhan, a Palestinian Arab, had trailed Bobby Kennedy for days. On May 18, he had written in his exercise book diary these words: 'RFK must be . . . be . . . be disposed of . . . d . . . d . . . disposed . . . disposed . . . d . . . of . . . disposed of . . . disposed of openly . . . Robert Fitzgerald Kennedy must soon die . . . die . . . die . . . die . . . die . . . die . . . die . . . die . . . die . . .' And die he did, late one night at the Ambassador Hotel, during the campaign. Sirhan, using a .22 Iver Johnson pistol, killed Bobby from the range of one inch, and in the melée escaped, only to be quickly identified and arrested.

The trial was a seminar for psychiatrists. Why did he kill? He was, or was not, mentally deranged, all the time, or at the time; or he killed with premeditation for a purpose, being in full possession of his faculties most of, or all of, the time. His diary showed that he had once worshipped the freedom-loving and liberalizing Kennedys, but they had supported Israel, the Jewish state which made him homeless, and in his eyes stateless. His mother blamed it on his Palestinian boyhood; how he had seen terrorism at work; how his brother had been killed by a car escaping hostile gunfire. Even in America he did not feel at home and wanted to make his mark for the freedom of Arab refugees by killing that remote figure who supported people or a cause which had rendered him homeless.

The Ever-Present Threat

Not just Americans, but the whole world may wonder where it will all end.

America waited until three Presidents had been assassinated before assigning to the chief executive a permanent secret service bodyguard, but this expert protection does not make the holders of the office of President immune, or frighten off potential killers. Two Puerto Ricans, Oscar Collazo and Griselio Torresola, set out on November 1, 1950 to assassinate President Harry S. Truman at his temporary home on Pennsylvania Avenue, Washington, DC. The White House was being redecorated and although Blair House is close to the official residence, within easy walking distance, the secret service agents insisted that Truman rode from door to door. On this day, Truman was having an afternoon nap when the Puerto Ricans, seeking independence from America, tried to storm Blair House. In a three-minute gun battle, more than two dozen shots were fired between the attackers and the guards, with the result that Torresola and a guard were killed and three guards wounded. Collazo, who later confessed that they had gone to Washington with one-way rail tickets, never expecting to return, was arrested, tried and sentenced to the electric chair. Truman, in a voluntary act of clemency, however, had his sentence commuted to life imprisonment.

Even President Richard Nixon received a taste of the death threat. While visiting Caracas, capital of Venezuela, a mob of 7,000, with a hard core of 500, chanting 'Death to Nixon', mobbed his car, and he had to escape with the help of secret service agents by abandoning his ceremonial route for the protection of the local US Embassy. He was then the Vice-President to the late President Eisenhower, but who knows whence the next attack might come? Who can say when for some other world leader, the assassin will strike and the world will once again stand still?

Right *Another American dream is shattered.*

Inset *Sihran Sihran – admiration turned to hate.*

Overleaf *Epitaph.*

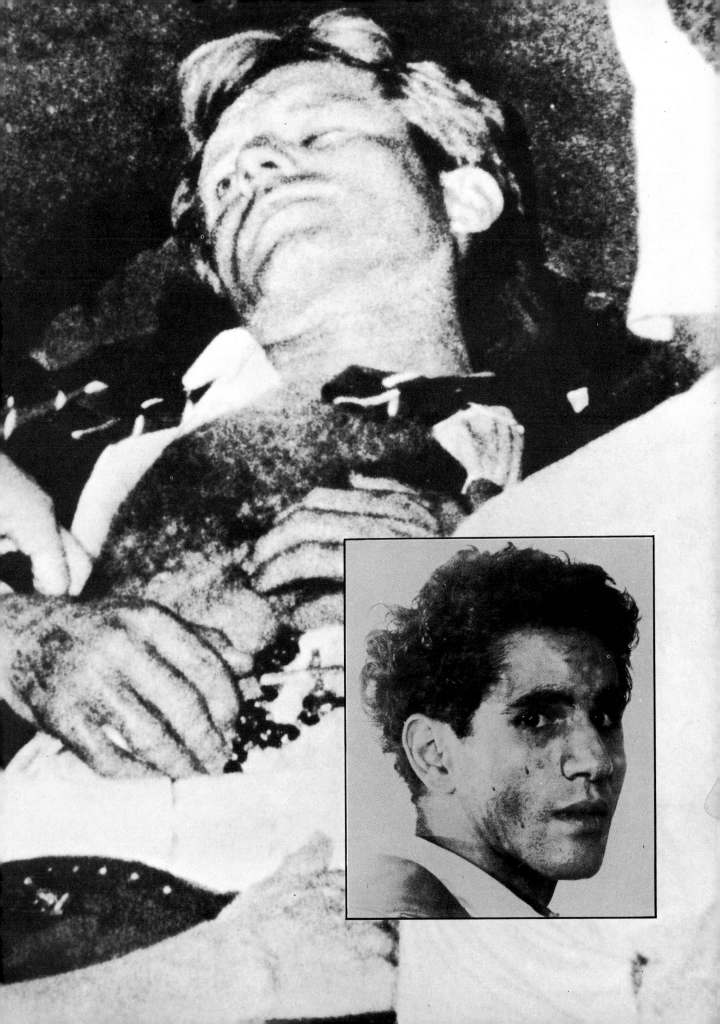